EYEWITNESS
PLANETS

Parker Solar Probe

A meteorite fragment
in false color

A young rocky planet
bombarded by rocks
from space

Jupiter's Great Red Spot,
captured by the infrared
James Webb Space Telescope

Ingenuity Helicopter

NASA's Perseverance
rover

EYEWITNESS
PLANETS

Written by
Carole Stott

Pluto, a dwarf planet

Saturn V rocket blasts off the launchpad

Earth's Pacific Ocean

REVISED EDITION

DK DELHI
Senior Art Editor Vikas Chauhan
Editor Ankita Gupta
Art Editor Aparajita Sen
Senior Managing Editor Rohan Sinha
Managing Art Editor Govind Mittal
DTP Designers Harish Aggarwal, Pawan Kumar, Rajdeep Singh
Jackets Designer Juhi Sheth
Senior Jackets Coordinator Priyanka Sharma-Saddi

DK LONDON
Senior Editor Carron Brown
Art Editor Chrissy Checketts
US Editor Jennette ElNaggar
US Executive Editor Lori Cates Hand
Managing Editor Francesca Baines
Managing Art Editor Philip Letsu
Senior Production Editor Andy Hilliard
Senior Production Controller Poppy David
Senior Jackets Designer Surabhi Wadhwa-Gandhi
Jacket Design Development Manager Sophia MTT
Publisher Andrew Macintyre
Associate Publishing Director Liz Wheeler
Art Director Karen Self
Publishing Director Jonathan Metcalf

Consultant Giles Sparrow

FIRST EDITION
Consultant Dr. Jacqueline Mitton

DK LONDON
Senior Editors Camilla Hallinan, Jenny Sich
Senior Designer Spencer Holbrook

DK DELHI
Senior Art Editor Sudakshina Basu
Editor Priyanka Kharbanda
Picture Researcher Sumedha Chopra
Picture Research Assistant Esha Banerjee
Managing Jackets Editor Saloni Singh
Picture Research Manager Taiyaba Khatoon
Managing Editor Kingshuk Ghoshal
Managing Art Editor Govind Mittal

This American Edition, 2023
First American Edition, 2017
Published in the United States by DK Publishing
1745 Broadway, 20th Floor, New York, NY 10019

A catalog record for this book is available
from the Library of Congress.
ISBN 978-0-7440-7993-7 (Paperback)
ISBN 978-0-7440-7994-4 (ALB)

DK books are available at special discounts when
purchased in bulk for sales promotions, premiums,
fund-raising, or educational use. For details, contact:
DK Publishing Special Markets,
1745 Broadway, New York, NY 10019
SpecialSales@dk.com

Printed and bound in China

www.dk.com

Earth-orbiting satellite

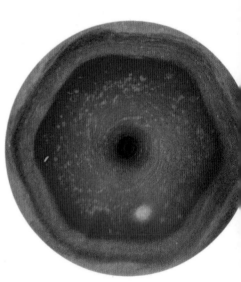

Close-up, false-color view of Saturn's north pole

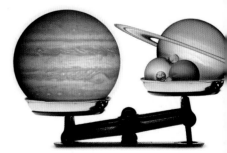

Jupiter outweighs all seven other planets combined

Contents

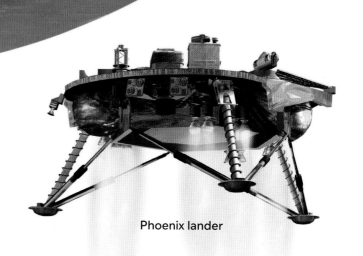

Phoenix lander

6
Planet Earth and
its neighbors

8
What is a planet?

10
Changing worlds

12
Skywatching

14
Space age exploration

16
The sun

18
Mercury

20
Venus

22
Earth

24
Water world

26
Living planet

28
The moon

30
Exploring the moon

32
Mars

34
The Red Planet

36
Roving on Mars

38
Asteroids

40
Jupiter

42
Jupiter's moons

44
Saturn

46
Saturn's rings

48
Saturn's moons

50
Visiting the giants

52
The outer solar system

54
Uranus

56
Neptune

58
The outer dwarfs

60
Comets

62
Exoplanets

64
Did you know?

66
Solar system facts

68
Timeline

70
Glossary

72
Index

Planet Earth and its **neighbors**

Part of the family of space objects called the solar system, Earth and seven more planets formed about 4.6 billion years ago. They each orbit the sun, as do billions of smaller bodies such as asteroids, and others far beyond the planets.

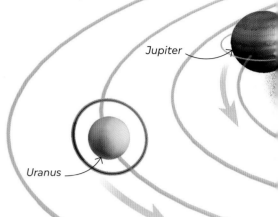

Jupiter

Uranus

Planetary solar system

The sun is our local star. Its gravity holds the solar system together. Following elliptical orbits—stretched, circular paths—around the sun, the eight planets and the asteroids together orbit in a disc-like plane that extends about 2.8 billion miles (4.5 billion km) out from the sun.

Inner planets

The four planets closest to the sun are also the solar system's smallest. Often called the inner or rocky planets, all four are balls of rock and metal, but with very different surfaces. Earth has life and oceans; Mars is a frozen desert; Venus has a volcanic surface; and Mercury is covered with craters.

| Mercury | Venus | Earth | Mars |

Inner planets

The sun contains more than **99.8%** of all **the mass** in the **Solar System.**

Outer giants

Known as the giants, Jupiter, Saturn, Uranus, and Neptune are the outermost and largest of the solar system planets. They are also the most massive, being made of the most abundant material—hydrogen. Each has a thick atmosphere, rather than a solid surface, and a ring system.

Jupiter   Saturn   Uranus   Neptune

Outer giants

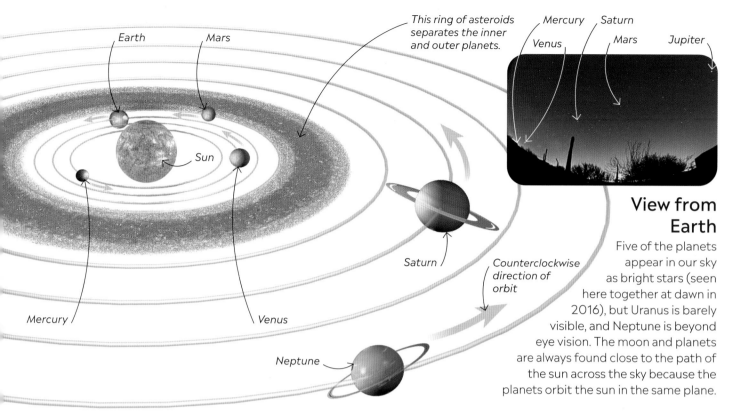

Earth

Mars

This ring of asteroids separates the inner and outer planets.

Mercury

Venus

Saturn

Mars

Jupiter

Sun

Saturn

Counterclockwise direction of orbit

Mercury

Venus

Neptune

View from Earth

Five of the planets appear in our sky as bright stars (seen here together at dawn in 2016), but Uranus is barely visible, and Neptune is beyond eye vision. The moon and planets are always found close to the path of the sun across the sky because the planets orbit the sun in the same plane.

The young sun starts to produce energy in its core.

A rocky planet forms in the inner, hotter part of the disc.

Planetary moons

Titan, Saturn's largest moon

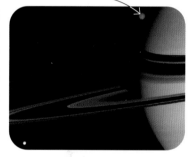

There are at least 219 moons in the solar system. Earth has one, and Mars has two; Mercury and Venus have none. All four giants have large families of moons—Jupiter and Saturn have at least 80 each, including Saturn's Tethys and Titan (right).

A giant planet takes shape in the outer region.

Birth of the solar system

The solar system formed from a spinning cloud of gas, dust, and ice particles. As gravity pulled material inward, the central region became denser and hotter, forming our star about 4.6 billion years ago. Unused material settled into a disc around the sun (above) and formed the planets.

Earth's axis tilts by 23.4°.

23.4°

Plane of Earth's orbit

Earth's spin is eastward (counter-clockwise seen from above the North Pole).

Orbit and spin

Most planets orbit in a roughly flat plane around the sun. Planets closer to it complete their orbits quicker than the rest. Each one also spins on an axis line between its poles. In most cases, this axis is tilted, giving rise to changing seasons.

STRUCTURE

Beyond Neptune is the Kuiper Belt of rock and ice bodies, including the dwarf planets Pluto and Eris. More distant still is Sedna, at more than 900 times the Earth-sun distance. Surrounding all of this is the Oort Cloud, home of comets, which marks the limit of the sun's influence.

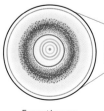

From the sun (center) to Jupiter (orange orbit)

From Saturn to Pluto (purple) and Eris (red)

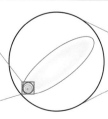

Beyond the planets, Sedna's orbit (red)

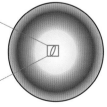

Oort Cloud surrounds all other objects

What is a planet?

For centuries, people have labeled Earth and other huge, round bodies orbiting the sun as planets. Recent discoveries have led to a formal definition, and two new classes—dwarf planets and exoplanets. Just as Earth and seven more planets orbit the sun, exoplanets orbit other stars. There may be tens of billions of exoplanets orbiting stars in the Milky Way Galaxy.

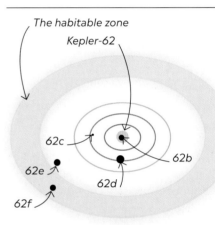

The planet Mercury—false color highlights different rock types

Defining a planet

The word "planet," from the Ancient Greek for "wanderer," was used to describe so-called wandering stars—planets moving across the starry sky. In 2006, the International Astronomical Union (IAU) defined a planet as a body orbiting the sun that is massive enough for its gravity to make it nearly round, and which has cleared other objects out of its path.

THE HABITABLE ZONE

The habitable zone

Kepler-62

62c

62e

62f

62b

62d

Kepler-62 System

Earth is in the sun's habitable zone, a region where liquid water can exist and allow life to form and flourish. Any closer to the sun, Earth would be so hot that its water would evaporate away. Any farther, Earth would be so cold, its water would freeze. Exoplanets in habitable zones could harbor life. Two planets, 62e and 62f, orbit the star Kepler-62 within its habitable zone.

Pluto with its moon Charon (upper left)

Dwarf planet

Discovered in 1930, Pluto was classed as a planet. But then Eris, a body more distant and seemingly larger than Pluto, was found in 2005. Both are far smaller than the other planets and follow elongated orbits among other objects. In 2006, the IAU introduced the class of dwarf planet. A dwarf planet orbits the sun and is massive enough for its gravity to make it round but has not cleared the neighborhood around its orbit.

The orange sun-like star HD 189733 has one known exoplanet.

Planet HD 189733b— a gas giant larger than Jupiter—orbits its star in 2.2 days.

Exoplanet

Exoplanets are small compared to their stars, which also outshine them—making them doubly difficult to detect. We know of more than 5,000 exoplanets. Most of those known orbit stars relatively close to the sun, but a few far more distant exoplanets have been discovered, including some floating alone in space.

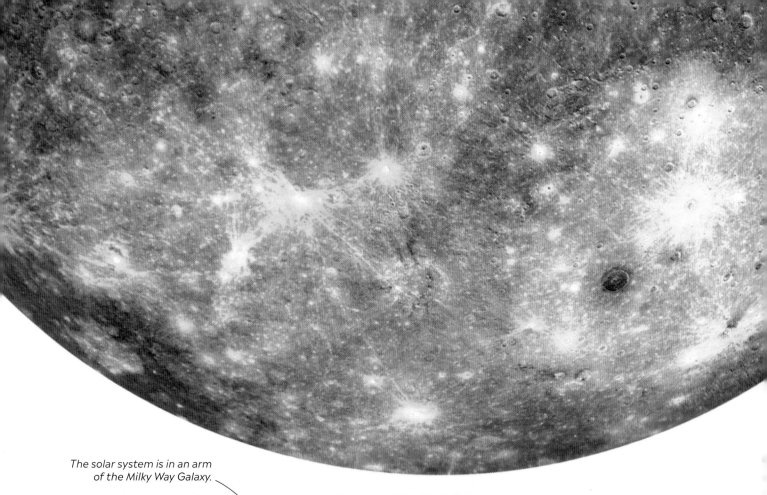

The solar system is in an arm of the Milky Way Galaxy.

The world of astronomy

While planetary astronomers look at planets in our solar system and beyond, in recent decades other experts have begun to look at the prospects for life on more distant planets. There are even projects underway to search for radio signals and other signs of alien life.

Our place in the universe

The sun and its planets lie within the Milky Way Galaxy, a vast system of stars, gas, and dust that has at least 200 billion stars. More than 2,600 of those close to us have exoplanets. Astronomers think at least one in every 20 stars has exoplanets orbiting it. And there could be as many stars with exoplanets in the universe's other 200 billion or more galaxies.

Giant dishes like this one in West Virginia may one day detect alien radio signals.

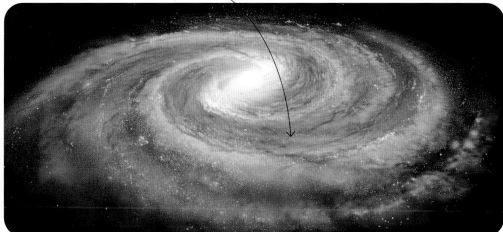

Naming the planets

The planets were named in ancient times after Greek or Roman gods, and we still use their Greek or Roman names today. For instance, Venus is named after the Roman goddess of love (left). Of the two planets discovered in modern times, Uranus is named after the Greek god of the sky, and Neptune after the Roman god of the sea.

Changing
worlds

Early in their history, the planets were bombarded by rocks from space that scarred the surfaces of the rocky inner planets. Over millions of years, volcanic activity, land movement, and the action of water, wind, and atmosphere have continued to shape the landscapes and features of the planets.

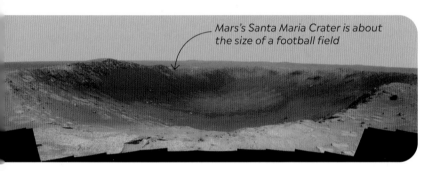

Mars's Santa Maria Crater is about the size of a football field

Cratering

Millions of impact craters scar the rocky planets and their moons. They form when rocks from space smash into the surface and gouge out material. The largest craters are hundreds of miles across. The rate of impact has slowed since the most intense period of bombardment, 3.5 billion years ago.

Rocky balls

The rocky planets took shape as material left over from the sun's formation clumped together into four hot, molten balls. As they cooled, they settled into layers, creating a rocky surface and metal core. More rocks from space crashed into the young planets, forming craters. Inside the planets, heat from radioactivity made the rock molten and some of it flowed out in volcanic eruptions.

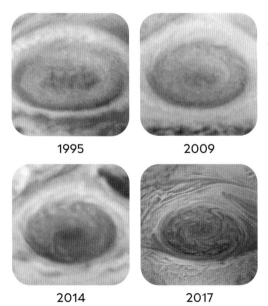

1995

2009

2014

2017

Giant planets

As the young giant planets shrank, their cores grew hotter and their upper atmospheres formed bands where storm clouds rage. In the last few years, Jupiter's long-lived Great Red Spot (left) has been shrinking by at least 124 miles (200 km) each year.

Volcanism

Heat from inside the rocky planets and some moons has powered different kinds of volcanoes. Over time, volcanic activity (volcanism) has tended to reduce as these bodies have cooled down. Earth is still volcanic, but its crust is thickening and volcanism will eventually stop.

Tungurahua volcano, Ecuador

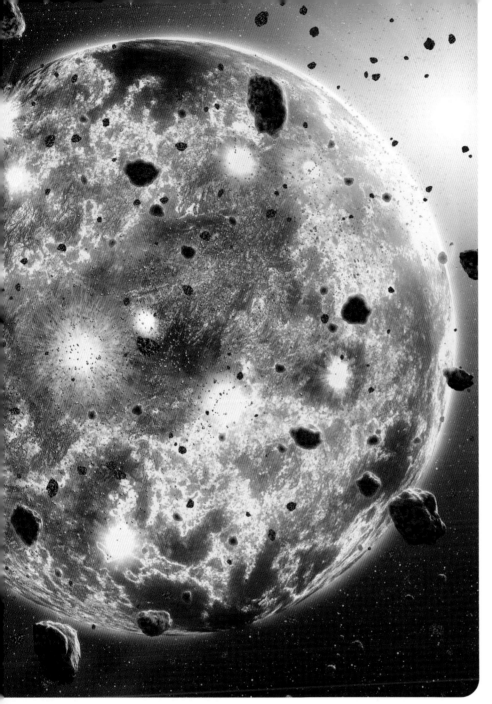

Hot Venus, cool Earth

Young Venus and Earth both had a thick atmosphere of carbon dioxide and water. Closer to the sun, Venus's water was broken up by the sun's energy, leaving a thick carbon-dioxide atmosphere (above). On cooler Earth, the atmosphere thinned as water fell as rain and carbon dioxide gas combined into rocks that locked it in. Much later, plants released oxygen into the air.

Surface building

The surfaces of the rocky planets are shaped by large-scale movements in their crusts over millions of years. As the young planets cooled and shrank, their surfaces cracked. Mercury's cliff Carnegie Rupes formed in this way. A false-color image shows it at the edge of the higher ground (red) cutting across cratered terrain (blue).

Erosion

Landscapes change through erosion—the wearing away of surface material by water and wind. On Earth, ocean waves change shorelines, rivers carve valleys, and glaciers pull underlying rock with them. Wind picks up material and deposits it at new sites. It also wears away rock surfaces, slowly sculpting new shapes (right).

Low land in Mars's northern hemisphere may have held an ocean of water.

Liquid water

As young Earth cooled, atmospheric steam condensed, water fell, and oceans formed. Young Mars also had liquid water in lakes and seas, but the planet has since cooled. Some water escaped via its upper atmosphere and the rest became frozen.

Skywatching

Humans have always watched the sky. The first people to study it made patterns from the stars and identified five planets. They observed the sun, moon, and planets moving against the background sky. The introduction of the telescope four centuries ago revealed many more space objects. Today, we know that the solar system is a tiny part of one galaxy in a vast universe of galaxies.

Heart of the universe

Earth was long thought to be at the center of the universe, orbited by the sun, moon, and planets (above). In 1543, Polish scholar Nicolaus Copernicus realized that the sun is at the center and that the planets, including Earth, all orbit the sun.

First observations

Ancient peoples used the sun's movement, and the changing shape of the moon, to keep track of time. Around 4,000 years ago, the Babylonians drew the first constellations—imaginary patterns around stars—and recorded the movements of the planets. At the same time, ancient Britons were completing Stonehenge (right). Its stones align with the rising or setting sun at certain times of year.

Sliding tube used for focusing

Using the telescope

Early telescopes—such as the one built by Italian astronomer Galileo Galilei—had lenses and were as powerful as a pair of simple binoculars today. From 1609, Galileo saw mountains on the moon, four moons of Jupiter, and Venus's phases. Modern-day telescopes use mirrors to collect the light from distant objects. The bigger the mirror, the more we see.

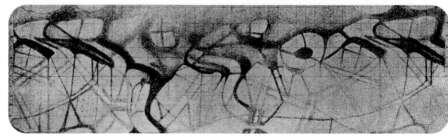

Surface features

As telescopes improved, they revealed details on planets' surfaces. In the 1870s, Italy's Giovanni Schiaparelli drew maps (above) of Mars's dark, linear features, which he called *canali* (channels). Others then mistook them for canals built by a Martian civilization—in fact, they are an optical illusion.

Expanding universe

Until the 18th century, the solar system was thought to end at Saturn. This changed with the discoveries of Uranus, Neptune, and the first worlds in the Kuiper Belt. We now know of many planetary systems in the Milky Way Galaxy, itself just one of many galaxies (below).

Sizing up the solar system

In 1609, German mathematician Johannes Kepler showed that planets orbit in an ellipse (an elongated circle), and those near the sun orbit faster than those farther away. Years later, astronomers worked out the masses of the planets (amount of material they are made of). Jupiter's mass is almost 2.5 times that of the other seven combined.

 EYEWITNESS

Henrietta Leavitt

In 1912, US astronomer Leavitt (1868–1921) made a crucial discovery without even looking at the sky. When comparing photographs of a star over time, she realized that the star's brightness could be used to calculate its distance from Earth. This later helped calculate the size of the universe.

Observatories

Several telescopes—each protected within its own building—together make an observatory. At their mountaintop locations, the air is dark, still, dry, and thin, giving the clearest possible view into the universe. The laser beam shown left shoots out of a telescope at the Paranal Observatory in the Atacama Desert, Chile.

Space age exploration

Buzz Aldrin on the moon, photographed by Neil Armstrong

Robotic spacecraft have been exploring the solar system since 1959. Far from home, in conditions no human could endure, they have investigated the planets, a host of moons, two dwarf planets, asteroids, comets, and the sun. Mostly about the size of a family car, they carry scientific instruments that test conditions on other worlds and transmit their findings home, making far distant worlds familiar.

Early exploration

The first missions to another world were the Luna craft sent by the Soviet Union to the moon. Luna 1 was the first to leave Earth's gravity, in 1959. Luna 9 was the first to soft land on the moon, in 1966. Lunokhod 1 (left) was the first rover to explore the moon. It landed in 1970 and roved across 6.5 miles (10.5 km) of its surface.

Lunokhod's cameras guided the driver on Earth who steered it around.

Mariner 9 started returning images of Mars in January 1972.

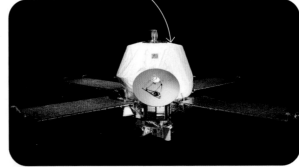

Mariner missions

Between 1962 and 1973, US Mariner missions made the first flybys of Venus, Mars, and Mercury. Mariner 9 (right) was the first craft to orbit another planet, arriving at Mars in 1971. The final mission, Mariner 10, was the first to visit two planets, Venus and Mercury.

👁 EYEWITNESS

Mae Jemison
US astronaut Mae Jemison (b.1956) broke barriers as the first Black female astronaut when she flew NASA's space shuttle *Endeavour* in 1992. She was one of the agency's first "mission specialists"—astronauts trained to carry out scientific experiments in space.

More than 33 robotic probes have now explored beyond Earth's orbit.

Sending astronauts to the moon

Twelve American men have walked on the surface of the moon, arriving two at a time on Apollo landing craft. The first, Apollo 11's Eagle, touched down on July 20, 1969. Just over six hours later, on July 21, Neil Armstrong became the first man to step onto the lunar surface, followed by Buzz Aldrin. Their trip to the moon and back was 953,054 miles (1.5 million km).

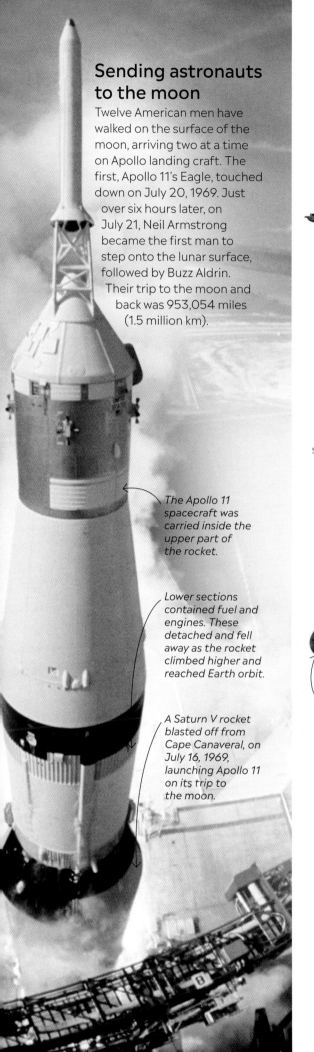

The Apollo 11 spacecraft was carried inside the upper part of the rocket.

Lower sections contained fuel and engines. These detached and fell away as the rocket climbed higher and reached Earth orbit.

A Saturn V rocket blasted off from Cape Canaveral, on July 16, 1969, launching Apollo 11 on its trip to the moon.

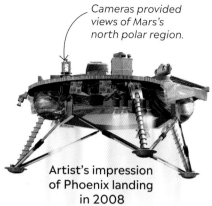

Cameras provided views of Mars's north polar region.

Artist's impression of Phoenix landing in 2008

Landing craft

Spacecraft use parachutes and small rockets to control their descent and make a soft (controlled) landing. The first soft landing on a planet was made by Venera 7 on Venus in 1970, but it survived for just under an hour in the corrosive atmosphere. Mars is more hospitable—four craft have successfully landed and worked there for longer periods.

Bristling with equipment

Each spacecraft carries a dozen or so scientific instruments, including several cameras, as seen here on the Curiosity rover on Mars. In this selfie taken by another camera, the large round eye is ChemCam, which includes a laser and telescopic camera. Below are two rectangular-shaped cameras, and at either side of them, a pair of navigation cameras.

Perseverance rover

NASA's Perseverance rover touched down on Mars in 2021, on a mission to search for past life and habitable environments. The six-wheeled rover is equipped with an array of cameras, drills to collect rock samples, and instruments to analyze the minerals it finds.

Each wheel has its own motor.

In-depth orbits

Spacecraft have orbited six of the solar system planets, from Mercury out to Saturn. By circling these worlds, they can make systematic studies of them. Whole planets can be mapped—and changes recorded—on a daily, monthly, or yearly basis. Juno (right) arrived at Jupiter in 2016 and moved into a polar orbit to start its scientific mission.

Three solar panels around Juno's hexagonal body provide electrical power.

The sun

Our local star generates vast amounts of energy, which is released into space and fuels life on Earth. Spacecraft monitor activity—from sunspots to huge jets of gas—and help forecast its effect on Earth. In the future, the sun will dramatically expand in size, destroying Earth.

Our local star

The largest and most massive body in the solar system, the sun accounts for more than 99 percent of the system's mass. It is a ball of hot gas—mostly hydrogen and helium—with no solid surface. In its core, nuclear fusion converts hydrogen to helium, producing energy that is most familiar to us as heat and light.

The sun's influence on life

The sun warms Earth and powers the water cycle (see p.24). Through photosynthesis, plants convert sunlight into chemical energy, as carbohydrates. These nourish animals that eat the plants. Photosynthesis also releases oxygen, which is vital to life.

Huge solar eruptions

Studying the sun

The sun is best studied from space, and a number of satellites continuously monitor it from a safe distance. The Parker Solar Probe (launched in 2018) has a daring orbit that takes it within 6 million miles (10 million km) of the sun's surface to measure conditions in its searing hot atmosphere.

The body of the probe can withstand temperatures of up to 2,511°F (1,377°C).

Solar wind

The sun constantly emits a stream of tiny particles called the solar wind, which shapes the magnetic field around planets and causes auroras. These spectacular light displays (above) occur when solar wind particles are drawn into the atmosphere above Earth's poles, collide with atoms, and cause them to give off light.

Sunspots

Dark, temporary patches on the sun's surface called sunspots are cooler regions where the sun's magnetic field interrupts rising heat. The number of spots varies in an 11-year cycle that also affects other forms of solar activity. The cycle's next peak, or solar maximum, is expected to be in 2025, and its next solar minimum will probably be around 2030.

A large sunspot seen in October 2014 could fit 10 Earths across it.

Coronal mass ejections

Made of billions of tons of gas, a coronal mass ejection speeds away from the sun (above). If it travels in Earth's direction, it can cause a solar storm. Solar storms can damage satellites, disrupt communications, cause surges in power lines, and trigger an aurora.

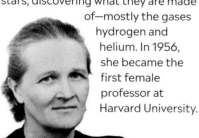
Solar eclipse

The sun's atmosphere extends far beyond its visible surface. Normally invisible, the outermost corona can be seen when the sun is eclipsed (below). A total solar eclipse occurs when the moon is directly between the sun and Earth, covering the sun's face.

In the future

In about 5 billion years, the sun will run low on hydrogen and expand, engulfing Mercury, Venus, and Earth. Before then, its intense heat will kill all life, evaporate oceans (above), and turn Earth molten.

Mercury

Sun-baked Mercury is the solar system's innermost planet. It has a huge iron core and a rocky, barren surface covered in craters. The sun shines seven times brighter than on Earth, but Mercury's atmosphere is far too thin to retain the heat, so it is freezing cold at night.

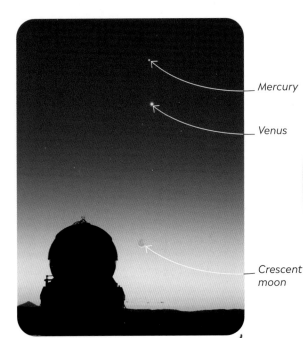

Mercury

Venus

Crescent moon

View from Earth

Mercury is never far from the sun in our sky and is usually hidden by the sun's light. But six times a year—during spring and fall—we see Mercury well, when its orbit brings it into view first on one side of the sun and then the other for about two weeks at a time.

Fast mover

Named after the swift-footed messenger of the Roman gods, Mercury speeds around the sun faster than any other planet. It takes just 88 days to complete one orbit. Yet Mercury spins on its axis very slowly, rotating once in just under 59 days, and completes just three spins in two orbits. The combination of slow spin and fast orbit means there are 176 days between one sunrise and the next.

The Amaral Crater was named after Brazilian artist Tarsila do Amaral.

Rocky surface

Mercury's rocky surface has hardly changed over the past 3 billion years. The impact craters found all over the planet formed when asteroids smashed into young Mercury. Its smooth plains formed when volcanic lava flowed over parts of its surface. Long ridges and cliffs are the result of Mercury's surface crust shrinking unevenly as the young planet cooled.

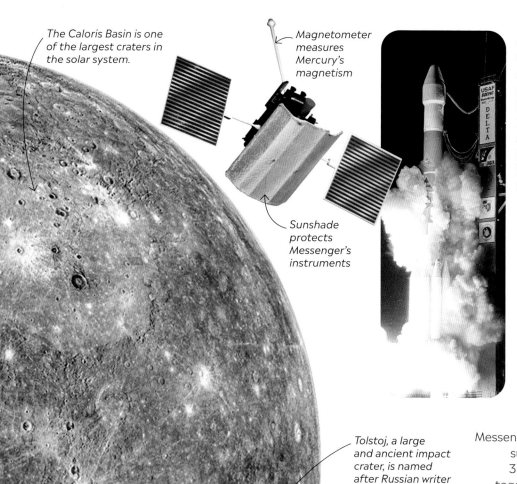

The Caloris Basin is one of the largest craters in the solar system.

Magnetometer measures Mercury's magnetism

Sunshade protects Messenger's instruments

Tolstoj, a large and ancient impact crater, is named after Russian writer Leo Tolstoy.

Bashō Crater is 47 miles (75 km) wide and is named after Japanese poet Matsuo Bashō.

Mercury is covered in craters—named after artists, writers, and musicians—because there has been no large-scale renewal of its surface since it was young.

Messenger investigates

Only two spacecraft have been to Mercury. In 1974–1975, Mariner 10 made three flybys, imaging almost half of the planet. Launched in 2004 (left), Messenger flew by Mercury three times before moving into orbit around the planet in 2011. By the end of its mission in 2015, it had mapped all of Mercury.

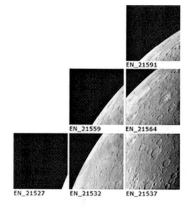

EN_21591
EN_21559 EN_21564
EN_21527 EN_21532 EN_21537

Mosaic imaging

Messenger's two cameras imaged Mercury's surface bit by bit. Each area imaged is 300 miles (500 km) wide. Once fitted together, the overlapping images gave a detailed view of the entire planet.

Caloris Basin

Mercury's impact craters range from small, bowl-shaped ones to the huge Caloris Basin, which is 960 miles (1,550 km) wide. In this false-color image by Messenger, dull orange highlights volcanic lava that flooded the basin floor. Craters that have exposed the original floor are blue. Younger craters are white.

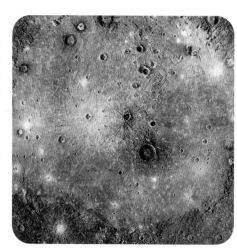

BepiColombo

Launched in 2018, the multi-part BepiColombo probe is due to enter orbit around Mercury in 2025. Its European orbiter will study the planet's surface and interior, and a smaller Japanese one will study its magnetosphere, the region dominated by the planet's magnetism.

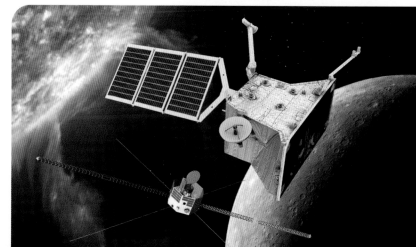

Venus

Almost as big as Earth, Venus orbits about twice as far from the sun as Mercury, but its surface temperature of 867°F (464°C) makes it the hottest planet of all. Its suffocating atmosphere hides a landscape of lava plains and volcanoes.

Atmosphere

Venus's carbon-dioxide atmosphere extends about 50 miles (80 km) above the surface. Its layers of cloud contain sulfuric acid droplets. Venus takes eight months to rotate, but the high clouds speed around Venus in just four days.

Venus has the thickest and densest atmosphere of all the rocky planets.

LOOKING THROUGH THE CLOUDS

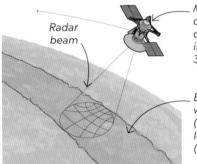

Radar beam

Magellan completed each circuit of Venus in less than 3.5 hours.

Each strip imaged was 10,600 miles (17,000 km) long and 12 miles (20 km) wide.

Orbiting Venus in 1990–1994, NASA's spacecraft Magellan used radar pulses to peer through the clouds. The signals that bounced back from the surface built up images in strips, which once combined, gave us our current global view.

Dali Chasma is a system of canyons and troughs more than 1,240 miles (2,000 km) long.

First surface view

The Venera craft were the first to land on Venus's surface. Venera 9 sent back a black-and-white view in 1975. In 1982, Venera 13 took the first color images (left).

Woman's world

This radar view by Magellan shows Venus's rocky surface, with huge volcanoes, lava plains, canyons, and impact craters formed in the last 500 million years, after the main era of volcanism. Venus is named after the Roman goddess of love. All but one of its surface features have women's names.

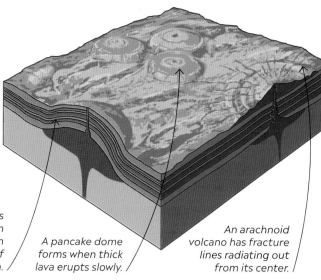

Shield volcanoes are built from a succession of eruptions of runny lava.

A pancake dome forms when thick lava erupts slowly.

An arachnoid volcano has fracture lines radiating out from its center.

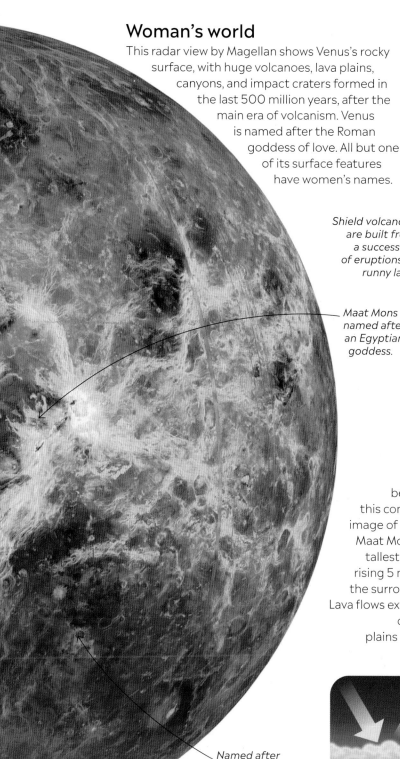

Maat Mons is named after an Egyptian goddess.

Named after Queen Isabella I of Castille, Isabella crater is 108 miles (175 km) across.

Volcanic surface

More than 85 percent of Venus is covered in volcanic lava. Hundreds of the volcanoes that released the lava are shield volcanoes, with gentle slopes built up by successive lava flows. The smaller arachnoid volcanoes, named for their spider-web-like appearance, and the flat-topped pancake domes are unique to Venus. Most of the volcanoes are thought to be extinct.

Maat Mons

Magellan data has been used to create this computer-generated image of the shield volcano Maat Mons (right). It is the tallest volcano on Venus, rising 5 miles (8 km) above the surrounding landscape. Lava flows extend for hundreds of miles across the plains in the foreground.

Greenhouse effect

Most of the sunlight reaching Venus is reflected back into space by the top layer of its clouds, making the planet bright and easy to see from Earth. A small amount of sunlight gets through the clouds, warming the rocky surface. Heat released from the rock adds to the warming process. The clouds work like the glass in a greenhouse, keeping heat in.

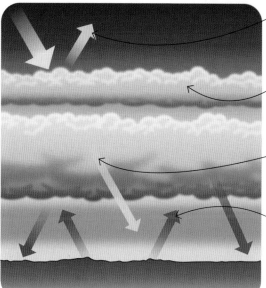

About 80 percent of sunlight is reflected off Venus's clouds.

The thick layers of cloud stop heat from Venus escaping into space.

About 20 percent of the sunlight reaches Venus's surface.

Radiation from the sun-warmed ground is absorbed by carbon dioxide in Venus's atmosphere and cannot escape into space.

Earth

Our home planet is unique for its liquid water oceans and the presence of life. The largest of the four inner planets, Earth is made of rock and metal and gets denser and hotter toward its core. Surrounding it is a nitrogen-rich atmosphere protecting life below.

Earth in space

In 2018, an environmental satellite GOES-17 captured this view of Earth, showing wispy white clouds, deep blue oceans, and pale brown continents of land that cover more than a quarter of Earth's surface.

INSIDE EARTH

Inner core

Crust

Outer core

Oceans

Mantle

Beneath the oceans is a rigid crust 4–5 miles (7–8 km) deep. Thicker parts—the continents—are 16–43 miles (25–70 km) deep. A mantle of rock below churns like thick treacle, heated by the iron and nickel core. The outer core is molten, but the inner core, though hotter, is solid.

Northern spring

Tilted axis

Winter in northern hemisphere

Northern summer

Equator

Northern fall

Orbit, spin, and seasons

Earth's spin axis is not upright, but tilted at an angle of 23.4 degrees. This causes the seasons. When one hemisphere points to the sun, it has the warm, long days of summer, while the other hemisphere points away and experiences winter. Six months later, the seasons reverse.

Aurora

Meteor streaks through the atmosphere

Thermosphere
81 miles (130 km)

Mesosphere
50 miles (80 km)

Ozone layer

Stratosphere
31 miles (50 km)

Troposphere
6 miles (10 km)

Atmosphere

Earth's atmosphere is mainly nitrogen and oxygen. Its layers are shown here with their upper heights. Clouds and weather occur in the troposphere, which contains 90 percent of the atmosphere's gas and is the only part with breathable air. In the stratosphere, the ozone layer absorbs harmful radiation from the sun. Beyond this, the atmosphere thins until it merges with space.

Tectonic plates

Earth's crust is joined to the top of the mantle, in the lithosphere. This is split into tectonic plates – seven large ones (left) and many smaller ones. Lying on top of the semi-molten mantle, the plates move at about the same speed that fingernails grow.

Eurasian plate
North American plate
Pacific plate
South American plate
Antarctic plate
African plate
Australian plate

The rock cycle

On Earth's ever-changing surface, rocks are broken down by water and weather, and pieces are moved by glaciers, wind, and water. Those carried to the sea compact into layers of rock. Tectonic activity brings rock to the surface as mid-ocean island chains, mountains, or lava.

Volcanic eruptions create new land through ash and lava deposits.

Snow and rain feed glaciers and streams, which erode rocks.

The remains of marine life and rock pieces compact to form sedimentary rock.

One plate under another causes a volcanic mountain range to form.

Metamorphic rock forms deep inside Earth as a result of heat and pressure.

Roof of the world

Where tectonic plates push together and buckle, mountains grow as rock layers stack on top of one another. The Himalayas (right)—Earth's highest mountains—took shape in the last 50 million years. The range is rising by up to 0.2 in (4 mm) a year, offset by weathering and erosion.

Water **world**

Earth's water makes our planet unique. Oceans and seas of liquid salty water cover about 70 percent of Earth's surface. Fresh water in lakes and rivers, as well as frozen in glaciers, ice sheets, and icebergs, brings the total to more than 80 percent. The movement of water plays a huge role in shaping Earth's surface.

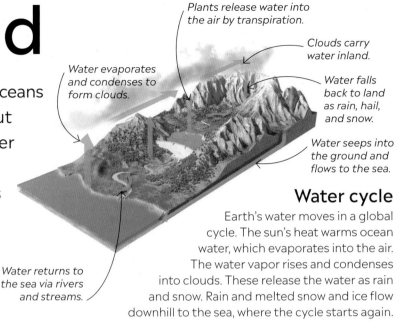

Plants release water into the air by transpiration.

Clouds carry water inland.

Water evaporates and condenses to form clouds.

Water falls back to land as rain, hail, and snow.

Water seeps into the ground and flows to the sea.

Water returns to the sea via rivers and streams.

Water cycle

Earth's water moves in a global cycle. The sun's heat warms ocean water, which evaporates into the air. The water vapor rises and condenses into clouds. These release the water as rain and snow. Rain and melted snow and ice flow downhill to the sea, where the cycle starts again.

Amazon River

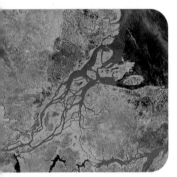

Rivers hold less than 1 percent of Earth's water but have a big effect on its landscape, carrying about 20 billion tons of sediment to the oceans annually. The Amazon (left) delivers a fifth of all river water reaching the sea.

High tide   *Low tide*   *High tide*

On this side, the moon's gravity attracts Earth more than water.

Earth's spin makes both tidal bulges sweep over the surface.

The moon's gravity attracts water more than Earth.

Daily tides

The moon's gravity pulls on the oceans. The pull is stronger nearer to the moon, so a bulge of water forms on the side of Earth nearest to the moon, and on the opposite side. As Earth turns, the bulges create daily changes in the sea level—our high and low tides.

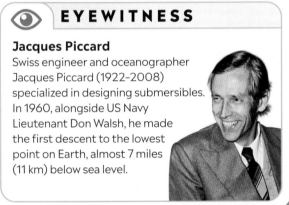

Frozen water

More than three-quarters of Earth's fresh water is ice—in glaciers, ice sheets and shelves (above), icebergs, mountaintop coverings, and soil. Most of it is in the ice sheet covering Antarctica—if it melted, sea levels would rise by about 197 ft (60 m).

The Hawaiian Islands rise 5.9 miles (9.5 km) from the ocean floor.

Hawaii, the largest island in the chain, is five merged volcanoes.

Under the oceans

The ocean floor is mostly flat plains, but it also has mountains and trenches. The Mariana Trench plunges 7 miles (11 km) below the Pacific Ocean's surface. The Mid-Atlantic Ridge is Earth's longest mountain range. Deep-sea volcanoes that break through the water's surface make islands such as Hawaii.

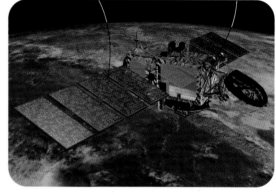

Jason-3 orbits 830 miles (1,336 m) above Earth, passing over the same point every 10 days.

A radar altimeter measures wave height and wind speed.

Water watch

Satellites orbiting Earth monitor its land, oceans, and ice. Jason-3 (above) measures the height of the ocean surface as part of a wider study of changes in sea levels and the effects of climate change. The Aqua satellite studies the water cycle, and CryoSat measures changes in the thickness of the ice sheets.

Blue planet

The largest of the five oceans—the Pacific—covers more than a third of Earth's surface and holds more than half of its liquid water. Next is the Atlantic, and then the Indian Ocean. The two smallest—the Arctic and the Southern oceans—are in the polar regions and have huge amounts of ice floating in them.

Myriad life forms

Earth teems with about 8.7 million species. Each species has its own set of characteristics that suit its own particular environment. There are almost 1 million species of insects, including around 40 species of leafcutter ants (above).

Living planet

Life began at least 3.7 billion years ago, and evolved from small bacteria-like cells to the huge variety we see today. Human expansion across the planet has contributed to the extinction of other life forms, and to climate change. Yet we are also fascinated by the potential for life on other planets.

Kingdoms of life

From tiny micro-organisms visible only through a microscope to Earth's largest animals—such as the African elephant (above right)—scientists group the huge variety of life forms into five kingdoms: animals, plants, fungi, protists, and monerans. Monerans are single cells with no internal structure. The protists are single cells but with a nucleus inside. Fungi include yeasts and mushrooms. The most complex life forms are plants and animals.

Beginnings

Life developed from very basic, self-replicating molecules into primitive cells. Multi-cellular organisms gave rise to more complex life such as plants and animals. Stromatolites (right) are layered-rock structures formed by single-cell microbes—similar ones existed on Earth 3.5 billion years ago.

Human impact

Global population growth has led to cutting down forests for farmland, destroying the habitat of thousands of species and reducing the conversion of carbon dioxide to oxygen by trees. As a result, the temperature on Earth increases, polar ice caps melt, and sea levels rise. Tokyo (above) is one of Earth's most populated cities.

Natural selection

Animals born with adaptations that happen to help them in a particular environment thrive and produce more offspring. Over time, this allows their adaptations to spread through an entire population, making it distinct from others. This process, called evolution by natural selection, was first observed by British naturalist Charles Darwin (1809–1882) during a five-year voyage aboard the survey ship HMS *Beagle*.

Extinction

Extinction is a natural part of the evolution of life. Some species adapt and survive events such as climate change or competition from other species, but many die out and become extinct. Many more species are extinct than are alive today.

Lonesome George, the last Pinta Island tortoise, died on June 24, 2012.

Search for life elsewhere

No evidence of life beyond Earth has yet been found, but spacecraft are searching for life on Mars, and Jupiter's moon Europa is the next target. Beyond the solar system, exoplanets in the habitable zone of their star might harbour life.

Part of the USA's Allen Telescope Array

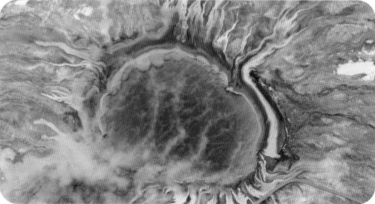

Extremophiles

Micro-organisms called extremophiles thrive in extreme environments such as scalding and acidic water. Fringing the hot waters of Grand Prismatic Spring (above) in Yellowstone, USA, are orange mats of microbes called archaea, which survive temperatures of up to 165°F (74°C).

The moon

The moon is Earth's nearest neighbor, a quarter of Earth's size, and the largest and brightest object in our night sky. Yet this ball of rock and metal has a dry, dead surface, with huge volcanic plains and highlands covered by impact craters. As it orbits Earth, it appears to change shape, from a slim crescent to a full moon.

Violent origin

About 4.5 billion years ago, a Mars-sized asteroid gave young Earth a glancing blow. Material from both splashed into space, forming a ring around Earth and then slowly clumped together to form the young moon.

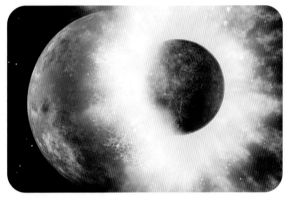

Lower mantle of partially molten rock

Mantle of solid rock

Mantle of solid rock

Outer core of molten iron

Inside the moon

Once the moon had formed a ball, it began to cool. Its heavy metals sank as rocks formed its outer layers. Today, the interior has largely solidified around a core of hot iron. The inner core is about 2,600°F (1,400°C), but it is squeezed solid by the rocks around it.

Crust of solid rock

Familiar face

The moon shines by reflected sunlight, and its surface features are easily seen with the naked eye. The near-side face (above) is always turned toward us. Its dark patches are areas of volcanic lava called maria. The lighter areas are older mountainous regions shaped by asteroid impact.

Tycho Crater is about 110 million years old and 53 miles (85 km) across.

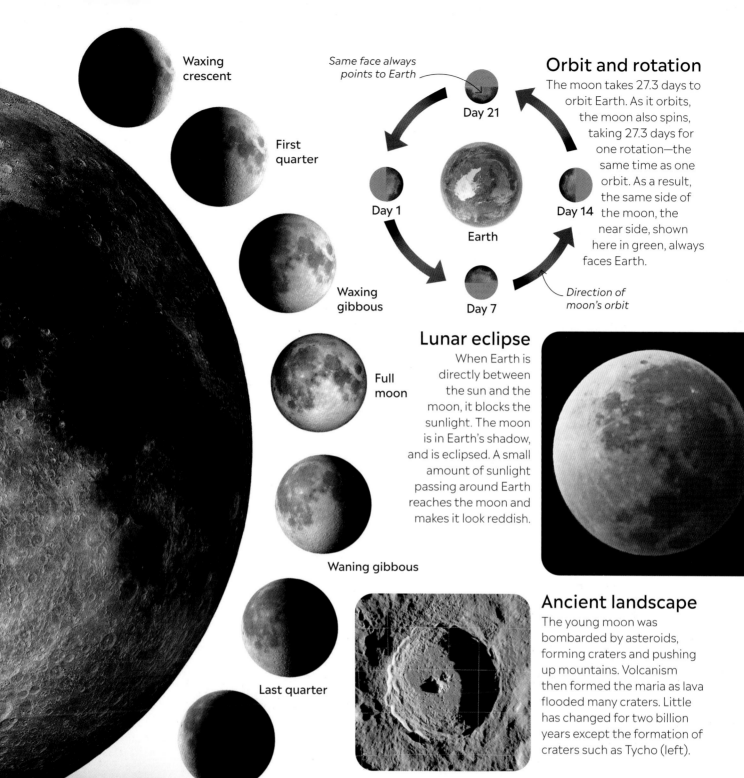

Waxing
crescent

First
quarter

Waxing
gibbous

Full
moon

Waning gibbous

Last quarter

Waning
crescent

New moon

Lunar phases
The moon's shape (or phase) appears to change day by day, according to how much of the near side is lit by sunlight. When the moon is between Earth and the sun, its near side is dark (new moon). As it orbits, the moon appears to grow (waxes) until fully lit (full moon) and then shrinks (wanes).

Same face always points to Earth

Day 21

Day 1

Earth

Day 14

Day 7

Direction of moon's orbit

Orbit and rotation
The moon takes 27.3 days to orbit Earth. As it orbits, the moon also spins, taking 27.3 days for one rotation—the same time as one orbit. As a result, the same side of the moon, the near side, shown here in green, always faces Earth.

Lunar eclipse
When Earth is directly between the sun and the moon, it blocks the sunlight. The moon is in Earth's shadow, and is eclipsed. A small amount of sunlight passing around Earth reaches the moon and makes it look reddish.

Ancient landscape
The young moon was bombarded by asteroids, forming craters and pushing up mountains. Volcanism then formed the maria as lava flooded many craters. Little has changed for two billion years except the formation of craters such as Tycho (left).

👁 **EYEWITNESS**

George Carruthers
US engineer George Carruthers (1939–2020) invented a unique telescope that was used to make some of the first astronomical observations from the moon. His ultraviolet camera and spectrograph, used during the Apollo 16 mission, was designed to capture energies from radiations that are usually blocked out by Earth's atmosphere.

Exploring the moon

People have studied the moon for thousands of years. Since 1959, more than 60 spacecraft have successfully traveled there. Six Apollo missions took 12 men to its surface between 1969 and 1972. It remains the only place that humans have visited beyond Earth.

Galileo and the moon

Italy's Galileo Galilei was the first to study the moon through a telescope. In 1609, he saw that it is not flat, as previously thought, but has mountains, craters, and smoother dark areas. His observations and sketches (such as the lunar phases above) became widely known.

Far side of the moon

In 1959, the Luna 3 spacecraft took the first images of the far side of the moon. Only the Apollo astronauts who have orbited the moon have seen that side in person. China's Chang'e-4 mission landed the first rover on the far side in 2019. The far side is heavily cratered, and because it had less volcanic activity, it has no large maria (lunar plains).

Men on the moon

In the 1960s, American spacecraft were sent to the moon to photograph the surface and soft-land on it. Once a site was chosen for a manned landing, Apollo 11 and its crew blasted off for the moon. Neil Armstrong (far left) and Buzz Aldrin (right) took the first-ever footsteps on the moon, on July 21, 1969, as Michael Collins (center) orbited overhead.

Rock and soil

The Apollo astronauts collected 2,200 rock and soil samples weighing a total of 842 lb (382 kg). The breccia rocks (above) formed when asteroid impacts melted and compacted the surface rock and soil. The basalts are volcanic rock formed from lava that seeped through the moon's crust, creating the maria.

Driving around

The last three Apollo missions—Apollo 15, 16, and 17—used a Lunar Roving Vehicle to explore a wider area. It could carry two astronauts, cameras, tools, and rock and soil samples.

Apollo 17's Eugene Cernan

The rover traveled at up to 11.5 mph (18.5 kph).

Luna landings

The Soviet Union did not land an astronaut on the moon, but it did launch key missions. Luna 9 made the first soft landing there, in 1966, proving that the lunar soil could support landing craft. Luna 16 (featured on stamps, above) was the first to return a soil sample to Earth, in 1970.

Return to the moon

Many spacecraft were sent to the moon in the 1960s and '70s, but none in the 1980s. Recent craft such as the Lunar Reconnaissance Orbiter—orbiting the moon since 1990—carry out scientific research. Japan, Europe, China, and India have sent craft, though the US will likely still be the first to return humans to the moon.

Lunar Reconnaissance Orbiter

Instrument looks for evidence of water as ice

Walking on the moon

The 12 men who walked on the moon explored six sites. Since the moon has one-sixth of Earth's gravity, they had to push off with one foot and float forward before planting the next. The final mission, Apollo 17, explored the moon's Taurus-Littrow Valley (left).

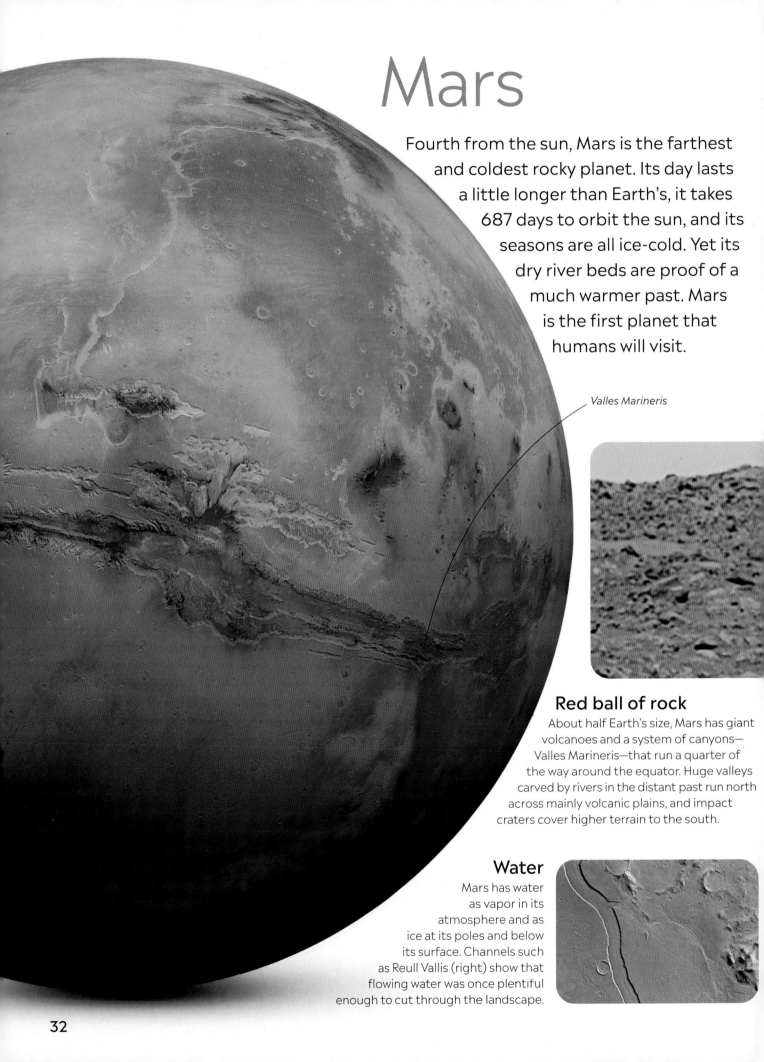

Mars

Fourth from the sun, Mars is the farthest
and coldest rocky planet. Its day lasts
a little longer than Earth's, it takes
687 days to orbit the sun, and its
seasons are all ice-cold. Yet its
dry river beds are proof of a
much warmer past. Mars
is the first planet that
humans will visit.

Valles Marineris

Red ball of rock

About half Earth's size, Mars has giant
volcanoes and a system of canyons—
Valles Marineris—that run a quarter of
the way around the equator. Huge valleys
carved by rivers in the distant past run north
across mainly volcanic plains, and impact
craters cover higher terrain to the south.

Water

Mars has water
as vapor in its
atmosphere and as
ice at its poles and below
its surface. Channels such
as Reull Vallis (right) show that
flowing water was once plentiful
enough to cut through the landscape.

Phobos is 16.7 miles (26.8 km) long, cratered, and covered in loose rock and dust.

Deimos

Phobos

Moons of Mars

Mars has two small, irregular-shaped, rocky moons, named after two sons of Ares, the Greek god of war. At a distance of 5,827 miles (9,378 km) from Mars, Phobos is closer to its planet than any other moon, orbiting Mars in just over 7.5 hours. Smaller Deimos is twice as far away and its orbit takes four times as long. Their origin is uncertain. One idea is that they were asteroids captured by Mars's gravity. Another is that the two formed from debris after a huge asteroid collided with young Mars.

A model of the Viking 1 lander, which tested its surroundings for signs of life on Mars with inconclusive results

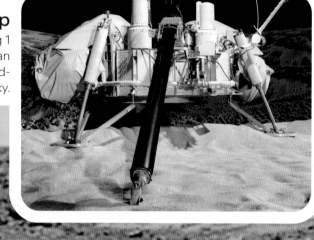

First close-up

Two identical Viking missions arrived at Mars in 1976. Viking 1 transmitted the first black-and-white image from the Martian surface, followed by the first color image (below), revealing a red-colored rocky terrain with fine-grained sand under a red sky.

Polar caps

Like Earth, Mars has a white ice cap at each pole. These huge mounds tower over the surrounding landscape. The northern cap is frozen water; the southern is water ice topped by a permanent layer of carbon-dioxide ice. Both caps extend in the winter and shrink in the warmer summer.

Mars's southern cap, named Planum Australe, is about 260 miles (420 km) across in summer.

Putting people on Mars

Space agencies and private companies aim to take people to Mars in the 2030s. Simulated missions on Hawaii (above) keep crews in isolation to see how they might cope on a round trip up to three years long.

Land has slid down the slopes and collected in the canyon floor.

Melas Chasma is the central and widest part of Valles Marineris.

The Red Planet

Mars is a cold, desert-like world with rock-strewn plains, hills, huge shield volcanoes, and vast canyons. Its rocky crust is in one solid piece over a mantle of rock. When Mars was young, the mantle was warmer and fluid. Its movement tore the crust apart, forming the largest canyons and volcanoes in the solar system.

Blood-red world

Mars's blood-red appearance in our night sky led to it being named after the Roman god of war. The color comes from iron oxide (rust) in the soil that covers almost the entire globe—winds sweep rusty particles up into the thin carbon-dioxide atmosphere.

Olympus Mons

Mars's biggest volcanoes are in the Tharsis Bulge, west of the Valles Marineris. The largest of all, Olympus Mons is 14 miles (22 km) high—almost three times the height of Earth's Mount Everest—and almost as wide as Germany. This huge shield volcano grew gradually as lava flows built up over millions of years.

Valles Marineris

This gigantic system of canyons is 2,500 miles (4,000 km) long and, on average, 5 miles (8 km) deep. Five times deeper and nearly 10 times longer than Earth's Grand Canyon, the Valles Marineris would stretch across North America. It formed when the Tharsis Bulge swelled with magma during the planet's first billion years, the nearby crust stretched and split, and land between the cracks dropped.

Fields of dunes

Dunes are common on Mars. They formed as wind piled up the sand and then sculpted it into different shapes. Some look like Earth's dunes, but others have less familiar shapes, such as long straight lines formed by wind consistently blowing in one direction. The crests of these dunes in Endurance Crater are less than 3 ft (1 m) high.

Craters within craters

Impact craters are found all over Mars's surface, but especially in its southern regions. Many to the north were covered by lava flows. The largest in this image is Hadley Crater, which is 75 miles (120 km) wide. Lava has flooded its floor, but later impacts each blasted deeper into the surface.

Red sky, blue sunset

Mars's sky is red because of dust particles in the atmosphere. At sunset, the sky around the setting sun turns blue as dust high in the atmosphere scatters sunlight. The rover Spirit captured this sunset in 2005. The Sun is white and smaller than in our sky because Mars is one and a half times farther from the sun than Earth.

If all the **ice on Mars melted,** water could **cover the planet** to a **depth of 115 ft** (35 m).

Roving on Mars

Out of more than 25 successful missions to Mars, 10 have landed on its surface, with six of these roving over the planet's rust-red landscape. Operated by on-board computers directed from Earth, and fitted with cameras and rock-analysis tools, the rovers record their findings and send them back to Earth.

Landing on Mars

Curiosity took just over eight months to travel to Mars, packed inside a protective casing. Lowered to the surface by a descent stage (left), it then cut itself free and the stage flew clear. Previous rovers bounced on to the surface inside a ball of airbags and then drove out.

Curiosity's selfie

Curiosity and Perseverance are the largest and most sophisticated rovers to have explored Mars so far, studying rocks and soil to learn about its past climate and geology, and to find out if it may once have supported life. Curiosity's self-portrait on August 5, 2015, combines several images taken by one of its 17 cameras.

THE ROVERS

The first rover to reach Mars, the US-built Sojourner, explored near its landing site for three months in 1997. The larger twin Mars Exploration Rovers, Spirit and Opportunity, arrived on opposite sides of the planet in 2004. The car-sized Curiosity has been roaming around the planet's surface since its arrival in 2012. It was followed by its near-twin Perseverance, as well as the smaller Chinese rover Zhurong in 2021.

SOJOURNER
July–September 1997
Distance traveled: 330 ft (100 m)

OPPORTUNITY
January 2004–June 2018
Distance traveled: 28.1 miles (45.2 km)

PERSEVERANCE
February 2021–present
Distance traveled: 7.3 miles (11.8 km)

SPIRIT
January 2004–March 2010
Distance traveled: 4.8 miles (7.7 km)

CURIOSITY
August 2012–present
Distance traveled: 17.5 miles (28.2 km)

ZHURONG
May 2021–present
Distance traveled: 1.2 miles (1.9 km)

Drilling into Mars

Spirit and Opportunity scraped samples from surface rocks for study, but Curiosity and Perseverance can extract samples from beneath Mars's surface using drills. The samples are analyzed to find out how the rocks formed, showing evidence of an ancient wet environment.

Flying over Mars

Shortly after landing, Perseverance released a small, four-bladed helicopter called Ingenuity (above). Ingenuity has so far made 32 flights using high-speed rotors to fly in the thin Martian atmosphere. It also helps guide Perseverance and identifies targets for study.

ChemCam's laser emits pulses from here.

The robotic arm, bearing the camera that captured this selfie, is not shown in full in this composite image.

Curiosity's ChemCam

The ChemCam instrument on Curiosity studies rocks and soil from up to 23 ft (7 m) away. Mounted on a mast, it uses a laser to vaporize the target rock surface, while a camera takes images. Another instrument analyzes the light emitted by the rock to determine its composition.

New explorers

Alongside US missions to Mars, other countries are joining the exploration of the Red Planet. China landed its first rover Zhurong in 2021, and the European ExoMars will be the first rover designed particularly to look for signs of past life. Perseverance is also collecting rock samples for return to Earth by a future US–European mission.

👁 EYEWITNESS

Diana Trujillo
After joining NASA, Columbian engineer Diana Trujillo (b.1983) worked on communications for the Curiosity mission and then took charge of the team running the Perseverance rover's robot arm. She is a keen supporter of programs encouraging women and minority groups to enter the space industry.

Investigating Vesta

Vesta is the brightest asteroid in our sky and the only one visible to the naked eye from Earth. Images taken by the spacecraft Dawn in 2011–2012 revealed the scars of collisions with other asteroids. One gouged out a large impact crater near the south pole and sent pieces of Vesta flying. Some landed on Earth, where they were collected as meteorites.

Craters cover Vesta in this view of its northern hemisphere, taken by Dawn in August 2012.

Meteorite evidence

This false-color microscopic view shows various minerals in a 0.2 in (6 mm) wide slice of a meteorite thought to have come from Vesta.

Asteroids

There are millions of asteroids in the solar system, with most in the Asteroid Belt between Mars and Jupiter. Left over from when the planets were forming, these small, rocky bodies follow their own orbits around the sun. The first asteroid to be discovered was Ceres, in 1801. More than 1.1 million asteroids have been identified to date.

SIZE AND SHAPE

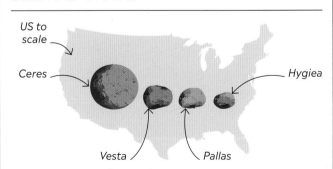

US to scale

Ceres

Hygiea

Vesta

Pallas

Ceres is 592 miles (952 km) across. As the largest, roundest asteroid, it is also classed as a dwarf planet. Next in size are Vesta, Pallas, and Hygiea. Only 26 asteroids are bigger than 124 miles (200 km) across. Others are irregular in shape and just a few miles wide.

The Asteroid Belt

The asteroids in this doughnut-shaped ring typically take four to five years to orbit the sun. Once the orbit of a newly found asteroid is known, the body may be assigned a name chosen by the discoverer. There are also two swarms of asteroids that have similar orbits to Jupiter and are named the Trojans.

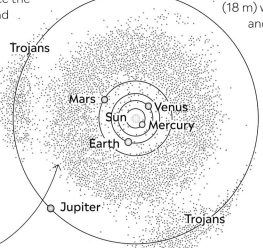

Trojans

Mars

Venus

Sun
Mercury

Earth

Jupiter

Trojans

Asteroid Belt

Close encounters

Asteroids that come within about 4.7 million miles (7.5 million km) of our planet are potential threats. Hundreds of the larger ones are closely monitored, but small ones arrive unexpectedly. In 2013, an asteroid 59 ft (18 m) wide broke up above Chelyabinsk, Russia, creating a trail of gas and dust (above). Larger chunks fell to the ground as meteorites.

Down to Earth

Tons of asteroid material reach Earth every day. Much of it is in the form of small pieces that burn up in the atmosphere. Pieces too large to burn up reach the surface and are called meteorites. Each year, around 3,000 meteorites weighing more than 2.2 lb (1 kg) land on Earth.

A meteorite weighing 2.25 tons (2,045 kg) was found in Saudi Arabia's Empty Quarter in 1966.

Impact with Earth

Large asteroid impacts on Earth are very rare. An asteroid at least 492 ft (150 m) wide strikes Earth roughly every 10,000 years and would produce a crater about 1.5 miles (2.5 km) wide. One of Earth's 190 impact craters, Pingualuit Crater in Canada (above), is the result of an impact around 1.4 million years ago. It is 2.1 miles (3.4 km) across.

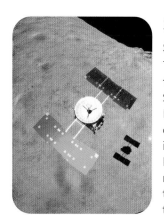

Studied by spacecraft

The first dedicated mission to an asteroid was NEAR Shoemaker, which landed on Eros in 2001. Hayabusa (left) collected dust from Itokawa in 2005 and sent it back to Earth. In 2020, the OSIRIS-REx mission collected rock from the asteroid Bennu for return to Earth.

Jupiter

The solar system's largest and most massive planet is named after the king of the Roman gods and ruler of the sky. Five times the distance of Earth from the sun, and the closest giant planet, Jupiter is made of mainly hydrogen and helium, with no solid surface. When we look at it, we see only the top of its deep atmosphere.

Giant world

Jupiter is made of almost two and a half times the material of the other seven planets combined, and 11 Earths would fit across its face. Yet it is the fastest spinner of all the planets, turning once in less than 10 hours. Its rapid rotation, fierce winds, and the large-scale movement of gases create the stripes that run parallel to its equator.

The Great Red Spot is the largest storm in the solar system.

COLORED CLOUDS

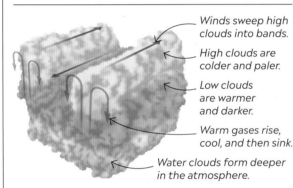

Winds sweep high clouds into bands.

High clouds are colder and paler.

Low clouds are warmer and darker.

Warm gases rise, cool, and then sink.

Water clouds form deeper in the atmosphere.

Hydrogen gas dominates Jupiter's atmosphere. The rest is mostly helium, with small amounts of hydrogen compounds that form the colorful bands of clouds at different heights. Warm gases rising from the lower, darker bands (called belts) form high, icy clouds in the paler bands (zones), then cool and sink in a constant cycle.

Comet crashes

Jupiter's gravitational pull can change the orbit of a passing asteroid, distort a moon's shape, or break up a comet. When comet Shoemaker-Levy was pulled into orbit around Jupiter, it was soon torn into 21 pieces that smashed into the planet's atmosphere in July 1994. Since then, short-lived bruises from several other comet crashes have been spotted in Jupiter's clouds.

Magnetic field

Jupiter has a magnetic field generated by electric currents within its body. This field influences a huge region of space around the planet. Solar wind particles and others from Jupiter's moon Io are drawn into the upper atmosphere above the poles, creating light displays called auroras.

Jupiter's auroras are hundreds of times brighter than Earth's.

Atmosphere

Liquid-like layer

Liquid metallic hydrogen layer

Solid core

Inside Jupiter

Jupiter's hydrogen and helium are in a gaseous form in the outer atmosphere. Inside, as pressure, density, and temperature increase, they become more liquid-like. Deeper still, the hydrogen swirls like a liquid metal. At the center is a rocky core.

Ring discovery

Jupiter's rings—discovered in 1979 by Voyager 1—are made of fine, dark dust grains from the surface of nearby moons. The grains are so thinly spread that the rings are almost transparent.

Winds in this dark belt stream eastward at 298 miles (480 km) per hour.

The Great Red Spot rotates counterclockwise once in six days.

This false-color image shows high clouds in pink, low clouds in blue, and the deepest ones in black.

Stormy surface

In the upper atmosphere, Jupiter's nonstop winds, fast spin, and internal heat stir up giant storms that we see as ovals. Some are short-lived; others last for decades. The Great Red Spot was once three times the size of Earth, but it would fit just one Earth inside it now.

Jupiter's moons

Jupiter is orbited by at least 80 moons and astronomers are on the lookout for more. The largest four are huge, round worlds in their own right, each with complex surface features. About a dozen are tens of miles across, and the rest are just a few miles wide and irregular in shape.

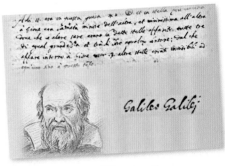

First discovery

Italy's Galileo Galilei was the first to see Jupiter's four largest moons, in 1610. They were the first moons to be found after Earth's moon and are known as the Galileans. Galileo's portrait and his description of a 1610 observation are on the Juno spacecraft now at Jupiter.

White areas appear where impact craters expose new ice

Ganymede

Callisto's surface is the most heavily cratered in the solar system.

Callisto

The Galilean moons

Ganymede, Callisto, Io, and Europa are known as the Galilean moons. Ganymede is bigger than the planet Mercury and is the largest moon in the solar system. It is an icy world—so too are Callisto and Europa. Io is the closest of the four to Jupiter and is covered in volcanoes. Jupiter's gravity distorts Io's shape and generates internal heat that is released at the moon's surface.

Ganymede's icy surface

Ganymede has an icy crust of bright and dark areas—the bright regions are mostly ice-tipped ridges and grooves, the dark ones, impact craters. Enki Catena, a chain of 13 craters that runs between the two areas, formed as fragments of an asteroid or comet crashed into the moon.

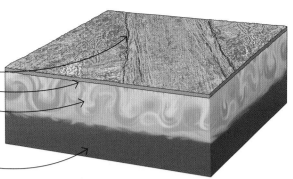

Ice-filled cracks called linea criss-cross Europa's surface.

Solid crust of ice

Warm ice layer

Liquid water ocean is about 62 miles (100 km) deep

Europa and water

The smallest and second-most distant of the Galilean moons, Europa is squeezed and stretched by the gravitational pull of Jupiter on one side and Ganymede on the other. An ocean of liquid water beneath its frozen crust is one of the few places in the solar system that could be hospitable to life. Ganymede also has an ocean, roughly 124 miles (200 km) below its surface, between layers of ice.

Volcanic Io

In 1979, US astronomer Linda Morabito (b.1953) was studying images of Io from the Voyager 1 mission when she spotted a crescent of light above the moon's edge. She soon proved this was due to a volcanic eruption on Io.

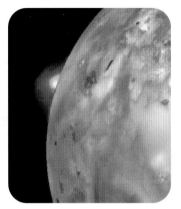

Triple eclipse

Jupiter's largest moons regularly travel across its face, but the sight of three at a time occurs only once or twice a decade. In this view by the Hubble Space Telescope in January 2015, Callisto, Europa, and Io are all passing between Jupiter and the sun, casting shadows on the planet as they eclipse the sun.

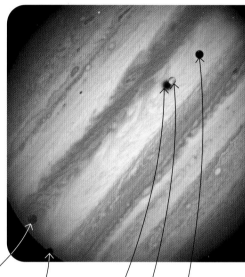

Callisto   Europa's shadow   Callisto's shadow   Io   Io's shadow

Io is covered by lava flows, and towering plumes of molten sulfur burst from its volcanic craters.

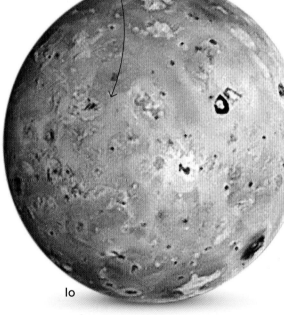

Io

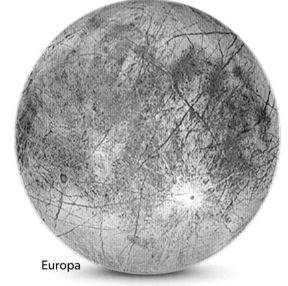

Europa

Io's tallest mountain, Boösaule Montes, is twice the height of Mount Everest at 57,415 ft (17,500 m) high.

21st-century discoveries

Many small moons have been discovered since 1610, and those identified since 2000 are smaller still. More than 50 have been detected by a team led by Scott S. Sheppard at the Mauna Kea Observatory in Hawaii (right). Averaging 1.9 miles (3 km) across, they orbit clockwise in the opposite direction to the Galileans, which suggests they are captured asteroids.

Saturn

In ancient times, Saturn was the most distant planet known, and marked the edge of the solar system. We now know this giant planet is the second largest, the sixth of eight orbiting the sun, with a wide system of rings and a large family of moons. The Cassini probe orbited Saturn from 2004 until 2017.

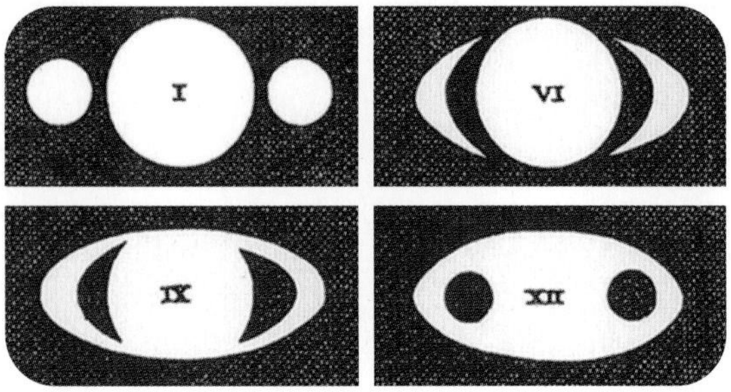

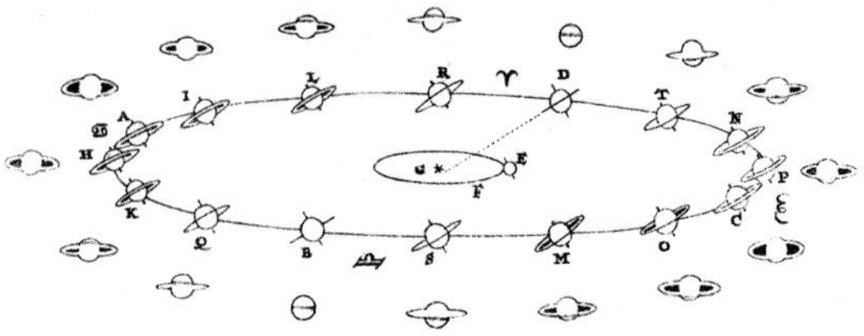

Early observations

When Galileo Galilei used his telescope to observe Saturn in 1610, he noted its strange shape. Galileo thought the planet might be flanked by two huge moons, while others suggested it had handle-like extensions or an oval shape with dark spots. Dutch astronomer Christiaan Huygens was the first to explain the true nature of the rings in the 1650s. His drawings of Saturn from his book *Systema Saturnium* (1659) are shown above.

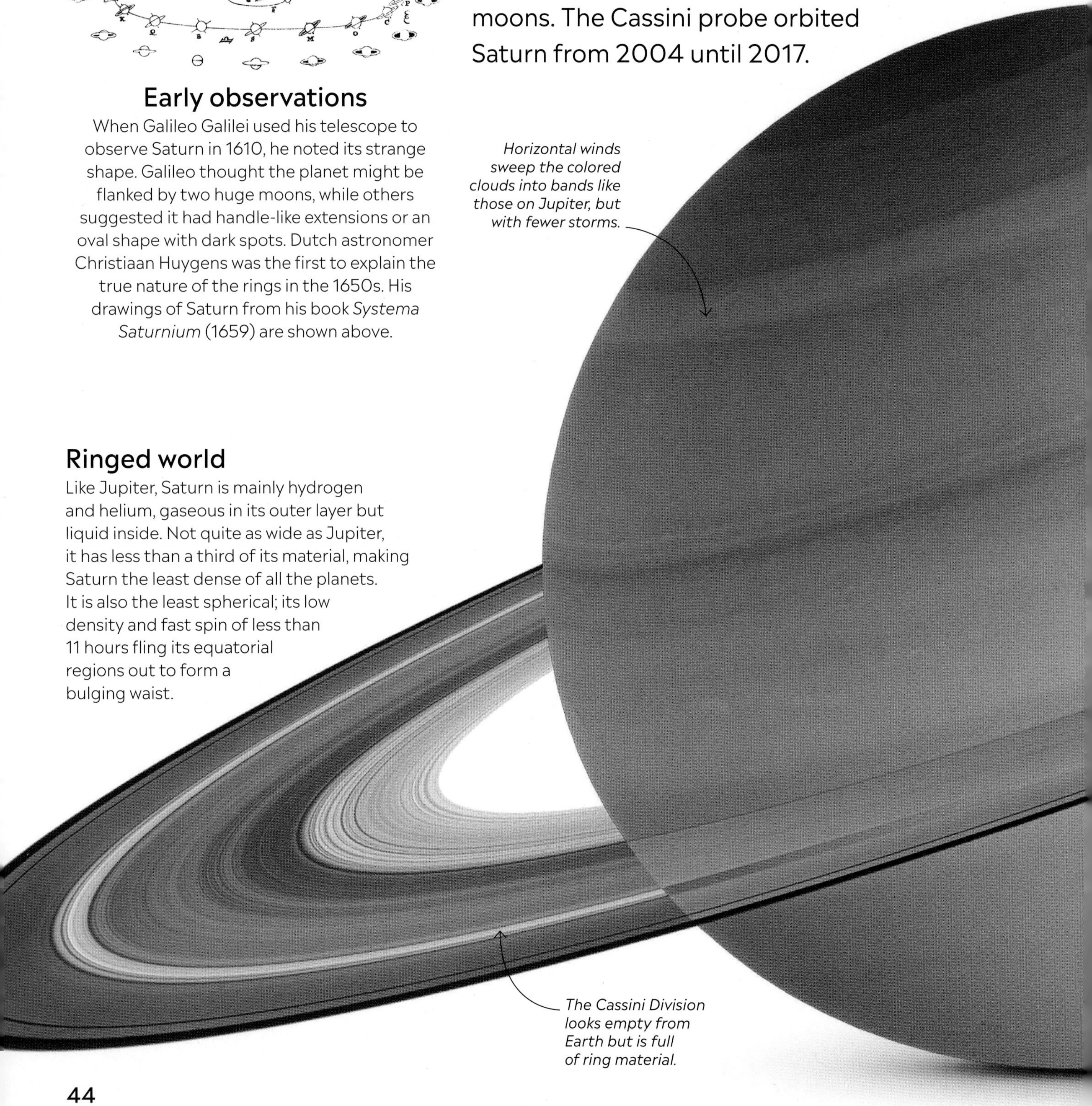

Horizontal winds sweep the colored clouds into bands like those on Jupiter, but with fewer storms.

Ringed world

Like Jupiter, Saturn is mainly hydrogen and helium, gaseous in its outer layer but liquid inside. Not quite as wide as Jupiter, it has less than a third of its material, making Saturn the least dense of all the planets. It is also the least spherical; its low density and fast spin of less than 11 hours fling its equatorial regions out to form a bulging waist.

The Cassini Division looks empty from Earth but is full of ring material.

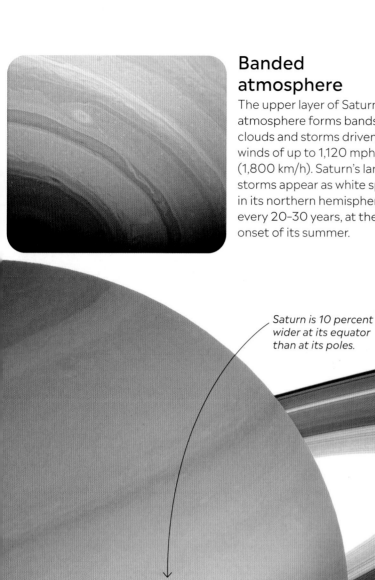

Banded atmosphere

The upper layer of Saturn's atmosphere forms bands with clouds and storms driven by winds of up to 1,120 mph (1,800 km/h). Saturn's largest storms appear as white spots in its northern hemisphere every 20–30 years, at the onset of its summer.

Northern storm

The most intense storm ever seen on Saturn took shape in the northern hemisphere in 2011 (above). Within three months, it had spread right around the planet.

Saturn is 10 percent wider at its equator than at its poles.

The central hurricane is about 50 times larger than any on Earth.

Polar regions

Saturn's atmospheric bands produce a hurricane-like vortex at each pole. The northern vortex (right) is surrounded by a six-sided jet stream that whips around at about 217 mph (350 km/h). In this false-color close-up, other storms appear as reddish or white ovals.

The view from Saturn

In this Cassini image, Earth appears as a tiny, distant, pale blue dot. Saturn is 9.5 times farther from the sun than Earth and takes 29.5 years to orbit the sun. It receives about 1 percent of the sun's heat and light that reach Earth but creates more heat internally.

Earth

45

Saturn's rings

The most impressive rings of any planet encircle Saturn. They are made of millions of orbiting pieces prevented by Saturn's gravity from combining to form a single moon. The rings extend to many times Saturn's width but average only about 33 ft (10 m) deep, and small moons sweep the gaps in between.

Keeler Gap

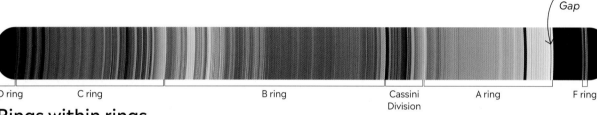

D ring   C ring   B ring   Cassini Division   A ring   F ring

Rings within rings

The rings most readily seen from Earth are named A, B, and C. Each consists of individual rings of material. At either side of these three are more recently discovered rings that are almost transparent. The D ring is closest to Saturn, while E, F, and G lie beyond the A ring. There are a small number of gaps between the rings, such as the Cassini Division. They look empty from a distance but are full of material.

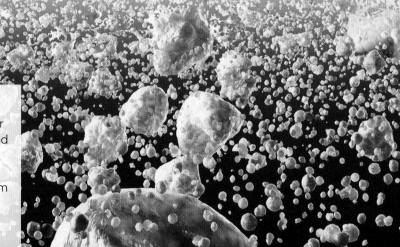

Icy particles reflect sunlight well, making the rings bright and easy to see.

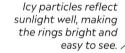

Ring pieces

The pieces that make up the rings are dusty water ice, and range in size from tiny grains to truck-sized boulders. Each follows its own circular orbit in a plane extending out from Saturn's equator. Their origin is uncertain. The pieces could be debris from a moon torn apart by Saturn's gravity, or from a moon destroyed in a collision with another body.

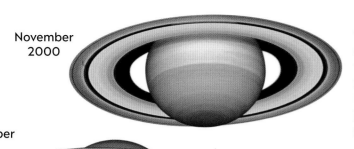

November
2000

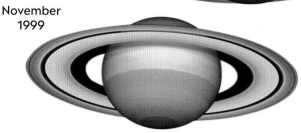

November
1999

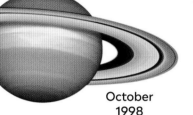

October
1998

October
1997

October
1996

Changing view

Our view of the rings changes as Saturn orbits the sun. The planet tilts by 27 degrees on its spin axis, and each hemisphere points toward the sun once per orbit. In these five views, more and more of the southern hemisphere faces the sun. The rings will lie edge on in 2025, and be wide open once again in 2032.

Ring peaks

The gravity of moons within the ring system causes kinks and waves in individual rings, or forces pieces into peaks. Cassini imaged these peaks rising up to 1.6 miles (2.5 km) above the edge of the B ring.

Tall peaks cast long shadows on the B ring.

Shepherd moon

Daphnis (right) is just 5 miles (8 km) wide and orbits within the Keeler Gap. It shepherds material into the ring and maintains the gap, causing ripples on both edges.

Giant dust ring

A huge new ring found in 2009 is tilted from Saturn's main ring system. Made of dust, it starts 3.7 million miles (6 million km) from Saturn and extends twice as far again. It is also very thick, about 20 times Saturn's width from top to bottom. Invisible to the eye, the giant ring is seen here in infrared.

Saturn's moons

Saturn's 83 moons range from Titan, bigger than Mercury, to more than 30 city-sized icy rocks. The planet has seven major moons, all of which are round. The bigger ones orbit closest to Saturn—some within its rings—while the smallest orbit up to 15.5 million miles (25 million km) away. All are icy worlds, but Titan is the only solar system moon with a dense atmosphere and liquid seas and lakes.

Explosive Enceladus

When NASA's space probe Cassini flew by Enceladus, it saw that huge areas have been resurfaced and that it is geologically active. Jets of water ice and water vapor burst through four long fractures in its crust and into nearby space. The water comes from subsurface lakes that could support life.

Hyperion

Some of Saturn's moons are irregular in shape. Hyperion, the largest of these, is 360 km (224 miles) long. This icy rock body looks spongelike—hit by other objects in the past, its surface material was blasted away. It orbits Saturn in 21.3 days, rotating chaotically as it travels.

Ithaca Chasma is a canyon system that runs for 757 miles (1,219 km).

Herschel Crater is named after William Herschel, who discovered Mimas.

Long fractures cut through the icy surface.

Mimas
The innermost and smallest of Saturn's major moons orbits in the Cassini Division.

Enceladus
This bright moon orbits within the E ring, beyond the main rings. It is 318 miles (512 km) across.

Tethys
Like Mimas and Enceladus, Tethys is made of water-ice and rock. It shares its orbit with two small, irregular-shaped moons.

Dione
Long, white streaks on Dione's cratered surface are deep canyons in the icy crust. Dione orbits within the E ring, with two small, irregular moons.

Seas on Titan

Titan's three large seas are all close to the north pole. Ligeia Mare (above) is the second largest, and contains mainly methane. It is about 311 miles (500 km) at its widest point, and up to 525 ft (160 m) deep.

Titan

The second-largest moon in the solar system is a cold world of rock and ice about 3,200 miles (5,150 km) across, hidden by a thick nitrogen atmosphere. Cassini's instruments revealed Titan's surface for the first time, showing a world where low temperatures create a methane cycle similar to Earth's water cycle.

Huygens probe

Cassini's Huygens probe parachuted on to Titan's surface and sent back data for about 90 minutes. The landing site was flat and strewn with smooth pebbles and rocks.

Engelier Crater

Iapetus

Iapetus takes 79.3 days to orbit, at an average distance of 2.2 million miles (3.6 million km) from Saturn. One side is dark, the other, light, with craters on both—Engelier, one of the largest, is 313 miles (504 km) wide.

Bright icy material thrown out by an impact crater

Rhea

Rhea is Saturn's second-largest moon—949 miles (1,528 km) across—and the first of the moons that orbit Saturn beyond the ring system, completing its orbit in 4.5 days. Rhea's icy surface is heavily pockmarked by impact craters.

Where are they now?

All four Pioneer and Voyager craft continue to travel away from the sun. The year of launch, and the year and distance when we last received a signal from Pioneer 10 and 11, are shown above. The Voyagers are still sending signals from beyond the planets.

PIONEER 11
(1973–1995)
4 billion miles
(6.5 billion km)

PIONEER 10
(1972–2003)
7.6 billion miles
(12.2 billion km)

Visiting the giants

The first spacecraft to venture beyond the Asteroid Belt and fly by the outer planets were Pioneer 10 and 11 and Voyager 1 and 2, which were launched in the 1970s. In-depth study came later, with Galileo and Juno, and Cassini orbiting Jupiter and Saturn, respectively.

Message from Earth

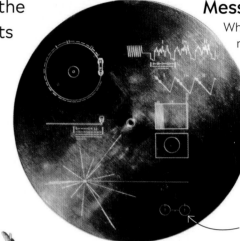

While the Pioneers carried a metal plaque identifying their origin, the Voyagers have a gramophone record that locates Earth and includes many of its sounds and images. Information on the cover (left) is designed to enable any advanced civilization to play the record.

Graphics show how to play the record.

The grand tour

Voyager 2 launch August 20, 1977

Neptune

Jupiter

Uranus

Saturn

Voyager 1 launch September 5, 1977

The Voyager craft left Earth in 1977. Voyager 1 flew by Jupiter and Saturn and was the first to leave the planetary part of the solar system when it entered interstellar space in 2012. Voyager 2 flew past Jupiter and Saturn and then past Uranus and Neptune. By harnessing the gravity of each planet, it swung from one to the next, using less fuel.

Sunshield

High-gain antenna for communication with Earth

👁 EYEWITNESS

Carl Sagan
US astronomer Carl Sagan (1934–1996) was involved in several of NASA's early space probes. Knowing that Pioneer 10 and 11 and Voyager 1 and 2 would continue traveling far beyond the solar system, he devised metal panels and records to carry messages to alien civilizations.

Galileo at Jupiter

In 1995–2003, Galileo (above) made the first long-term study of Jupiter in close-up, with 35 orbits of the planet and flybys of its Galilean moons. It also released a probe into Jupiter's atmosphere. At the end of the mission, it destroyed itself by plunging into Jupiter to avoid contaminating its moons.

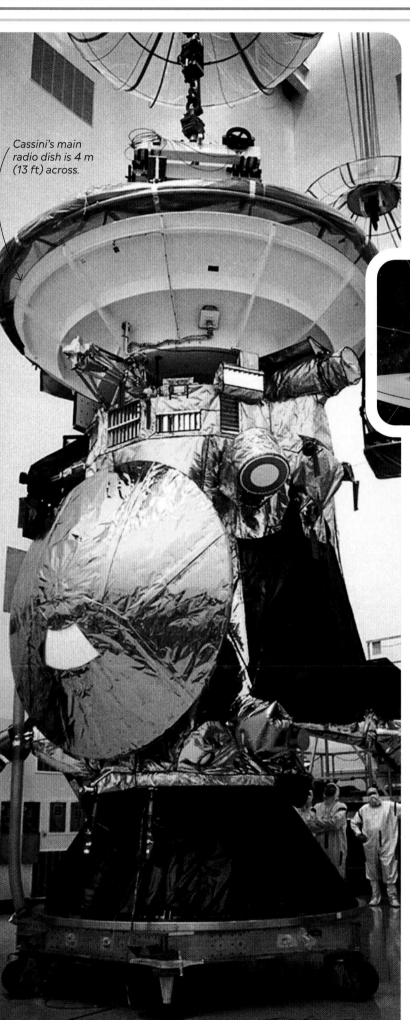

Cassini's main radio dish is 4 m (13 ft) across.

VOYAGER 2
(1977–ongoing)
12.1 billion miles
(19.5 billion km)

VOYAGER 1
(1977–ongoing)
14.6 billion miles
(23.5 billion km)

Cassini's mission to Saturn

The size of a bus, Cassini is the largest and most complex craft sent to a planet. In 2004, it started orbiting Saturn (below). On an early flyby of Titan, it released the Huygens probe on to the moon's surface. Its mission ended in 2017, after 20 years of service—7 traveling to Saturn and 13 in orbit.

Cassini recorded ring particles and temperature as it orbited Saturn.

Holes in the probe's cover let in atmospheric gas for analysis.

Huygens' descent to Titan

On release by Cassini, Huygens' main parachute opened to slow its descent to Titan. As its heat shield fell away, the probe began to test the atmosphere and image the moon's surface. It transmitted data as it fell and for about 1.5 hours after landing.

A closer look

The Juno mission arrived at Jupiter in 2016, entering a highly elongated orbit that flies within 2,600 miles (4,200 km) of the planet's poles. This allows it to study Jupiter's magnetic and gravitational fields, while reducing the damage from belts of radiation near its equator.

The outer solar system

The first object discovered beyond Saturn was Uranus, in 1781. Today, we know the dark and cold outer region of the solar system contains billions of objects—not only the planets Uranus and Neptune but dwarf planets and a ring of Kuiper Belt objects, too. Beyond, surrounding all of this, lies the Oort Cloud of deep-frozen comet nuclei.

The Kuiper Belt is 30–50 times farther from the sun than Earth is.

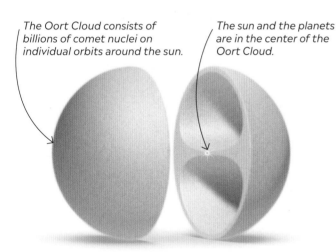

The Oort Cloud consists of billions of comet nuclei on individual orbits around the sun.

The sun and the planets are in the center of the Oort Cloud.

Beyond Saturn

The eight planets orbit the sun in roughly the same plane, making a disc-shaped system. Beyond is the Kuiper Belt, a flattened belt thought to contain hundreds of thousands of ice-and-rock bodies. Many of these, such as Pluto, follow orbits that take them out of the planetary plane. The Belt and the Oort Cloud are made up of material left over after the planets formed at the dawn of the solar system.

The Oort Cloud

The vast Oort Cloud is a reservoir of comet nuclei that follow elongated paths around the sun in all directions. As a group, they form the spherical Oort Cloud, which surrounds the rest of the solar system. The outer edge of the cloud is about 100,000 times more distant from the sun than Earth is and stretches halfway to the nearest stars.

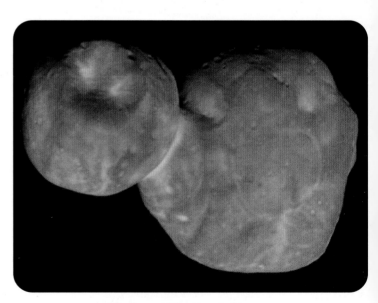

Planet discovery

William Herschel (left) was a German-born astronomer. When he found Uranus in 1781, no one knew planets existed beyond Saturn. Scientists then realized that something was pulling on Uranus as it orbited the sun and predicted the likely location of a more distant planet. In 1846, German astronomer Johann Galle discovered Neptune.

Kuiper Belt objects

More than 2,000 ice-and-rock bodies are known in the Kuiper Belt. Most are classed as Kuiper Belt objects (KBOs), some are comet nuclei, and the largest are dwarf planets such as Pluto. In 2019, the New Horizons probe sent back close-up views of a KBO called Arrokoth (above). They showed that it was made of two smaller objects that had gently collided and had a reddish surface due to long exposure to the sun's weak radiation.

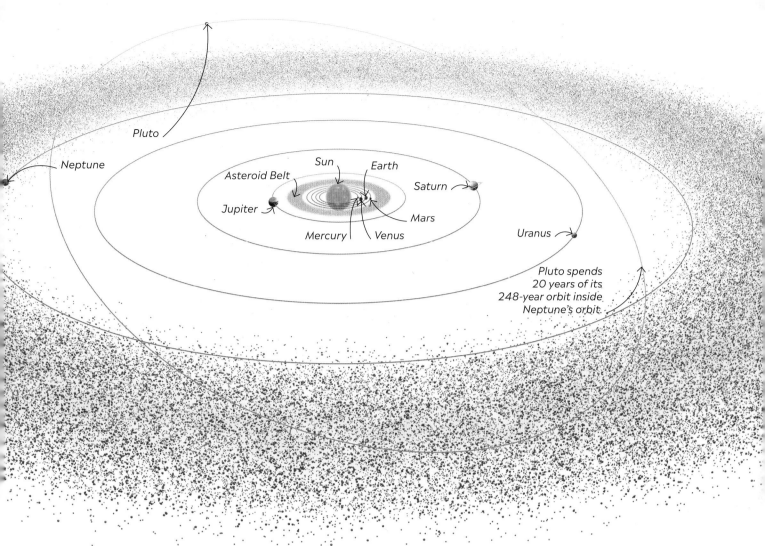

Pluto

Neptune

Asteroid Belt

Sun

Earth

Saturn

Jupiter

Mars

Mercury

Venus

Uranus

Pluto spends 20 years of its 248-year orbit inside Neptune's orbit.

Makemake is about 889 miles (1,430 km) across and has a moon.

What's in a name?

Some astronomers refer to the Kuiper Belt and Oort Cloud as the Edgeworth-Kuiper Belt and Öpik-Oort Cloud. Kenneth Edgeworth predicted a belt in 1943—in 1951, Gerard Kuiper came up with a similar idea. Ernst Öpik suggested the cloud of comets in 1932. Jan Oort (right) revived the idea in the 1950s.

Dwarf planets

The first solar system body known beyond Neptune was Pluto. Classed as a planet after its discovery in 1930, Pluto differed from the others in size, makeup, and orbit, and has a huge moon, Charon. Pluto is now classed as one of four dwarf planets in the Kuiper Belt. The others are Eris, Haumea, and Makemake (above).

Charon

Pluto

Artist's impression of the view from Sedna

Most distant

Some objects follow orbits out beyond the Kuiper Belt. Like Eris, they could be dwarf planets, or also be the first inner Oort Cloud objects to be found. Sedna (left) is 90 times the Earth–sun distance. The farthest known is 2018AG37, at more than 132 times the Earth–sun distance.

Uranus

Barely visible to the naked eye, and twice as far from the sun as its inner neighbor Saturn, Uranus is a freezing cold world. Only Voyager 2 has visited this ice giant, flying by in 1986. Spinning on its side as it makes its 84-year orbit of the sun, Uranus has faint, dark rings and 27 moons, which are much smaller than Earth's moon.

Some parts of Uranus's atmosphere are –371°F (–224°C) colder than any other planet.

Pale blue ball

Uranus is four times the width of Earth and is the solar system's third-largest planet. It is made mainly of water, ammonia, and methane. They form a slushy liquid mantle around a core of molten iron and magma. The outer layer is an atmosphere of hydrogen and helium. Methane gas in the atmosphere absorbs the red wavelengths of incoming sunlight and gives Uranus its blue coloring.

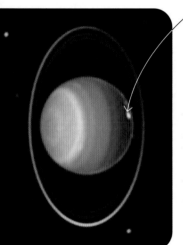

Clouds appear white, and pink around the planet's edge represents a high-altitude haze.

Bright clouds

When Voyager 2 flew by, the south pole faced the sun and the planet looked featureless. But when the equator faces the sun, new parts of Uranus are warmed up and it becomes a dynamic world. Infrared imaging (left) highlights its banded structure and bright clouds.

Tilted planet

Uranus's spin axis is tilted at almost right angles to its orbit, so it rolls along its path like a ball. Its rings and moons seem to orbit it from top to bottom. During the planet's orbit, each pole points once to the sun, receiving 42 years of sunlight, followed by 42 years of darkness.

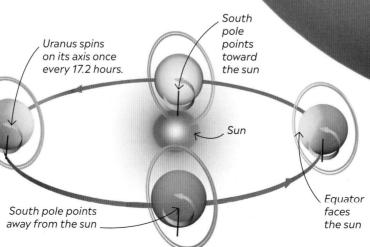

Uranus spins on its axis once every 17.2 hours.

South pole points toward the sun

Sun

South pole points away from the sun

Equator faces the sun

The inner rings consist of dust and dark, rocky material from a few centimeters to several feet across.

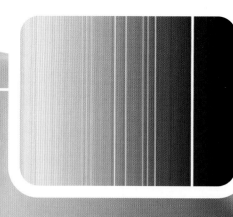

Inner and outer rings

Uranus has 13 narrow rings made of dust and dark, rocky material—11 form an inner ring system, and two are more distant. In this false-color image of the inner rings, the bright white one is Epsilon, the farthest from Uranus. Closer and thinner rings, just a few miles across, are pale green, pale blue, and cream.

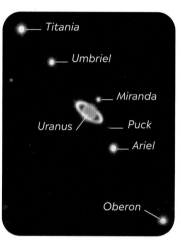

Titania
Umbriel
Miranda
Uranus
Puck
Ariel
Oberon

Moons

Only Uranus's five largest moons are roughly spherical. From largest to smallest, they are Titania, Oberon, Umbriel, Ariel, and Miranda. The other 22 are smaller and irregular in shape. The closest orbit Uranus in just hours, while the five largest take between one and 13 days, and the farthest take years. Tiny Puck, just 101 miles (162 km) across, orbits in 18 hours.

Clouds of ammonia, frozen methane, and frozen water droplets in the atmosphere

Titania

The largest of Uranus's moons, Titania is just under half the size of Earth's moon. Its icy surface is marked by impact craters and long canyon systems—cracks that formed when the young moon expanded.

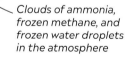

Gertrude Crater is Titania's largest.

Miranda

The smallest, innermost of the major moons is crisscrossed by ridges and canyons, and has the solar system's tallest cliff. Verona Rupes (above) is almost 6 miles (10 km) high. Some think it formed when the moon split apart after a colossal collision and came together again.

Neptune

The most distant planet in the solar system, Neptune is 30 times farther from the sun than Earth. It was also the last to be discovered, in 1846, and the last to be visited by a spacecraft, Voyager 2 in 1989. Neptune has the longest orbital path around the sun, completing just one 165-year orbit since its discovery.

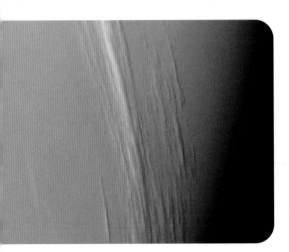

Deep blue world

Neptune is an ice giant like Uranus and is made of mainly water, ammonia, and methane. Beneath its atmosphere is a slushy layer of liquid and ice, and deep inside is a core of rock and iron. It is a little smaller than Uranus but more massive, due to its thinner atmosphere and deeper liquid layer. Its spin axis is tilted at a similar angle to Earth's, and it experiences seasons – each lasting about 40 years.

Atmosphere

Neptune's atmosphere is mainly hydrogen and helium, with water, ammonia, and methane increasing with depth. Fast winds whip around the planet at up to 1,300 mph (2,100 km/h), 10 times faster than hurricanes on Earth, and clouds sporadically appear.

Methane ice strongly reflects heat radiation seen by JWST

Neptune's rings and storms, as seen by the James Webb Space Telescope (JWST)

Dark spots

Huge storms on Neptune appear as dark spots. The Great Dark Spot—seen by Voyager 2 in 1989—was almost as big as Earth, but disappeared a few years later. A spot the size of the United States appeared in May 2016 (left, captured by the Hubble Space Telescope).

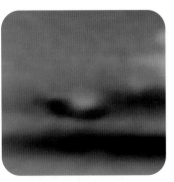

Dark spot with white clouds above it

Rings

Neptune's five dark, dusty rings are difficult to see except when lit by the sun from behind. Their presence had been predicted, but it was Voyager 2's flyby that confirmed the rings' existence. It also found the moon Despina, shepherding particles in the Le Verrier ring, and Galatea, which shepherds particles in the brighter outer Adams ring.

Triton

About three-quarters the size of our moon, Triton is a ball of rock and ice and orbits Neptune in less than six days. Its surface temperature of –391°F (–235°C) is one of the coldest in the solar system. Pink methane ice is found near its south pole (right).

Plumes of nitrogen gas and dust reach 5 miles (8 km) above Triton's surface.

Ice volcanism

Triton is ice-cold but volcanically active. Voyager 2's images of the surface revealed smooth plains of volcanic ice, and mounds and pits formed by icy lava. Beneath is a mantle of ice that erupts through surface cracks. Heated by the sun, the nitrogen ice turns to gas, and plumes of gas and dust jet up high above the surface.

Methane gas in the atmosphere absorbs red wavelengths in sunlight, giving Neptune its blue color.

Moons

Neptune's 14 moons are mostly small and irregular, but Triton is spherical and 1,682 miles (2,707 km) wide. It was discovered in 1846, just a couple of weeks after Neptune, but no others were found until Nereid, in 1949. The latest and smallest, Hippocamp, was discovered in 2013 by the Hubble Space Telescope.

Methane ice clouds in the atmosphere change their appearance in hours.

Hippocamp · Psamathe · Laomedeia · Sao · Neso · Halimede · Naiad · Thalassa · Despina · Galatea · Larissa · Nereid · Proteus · Triton

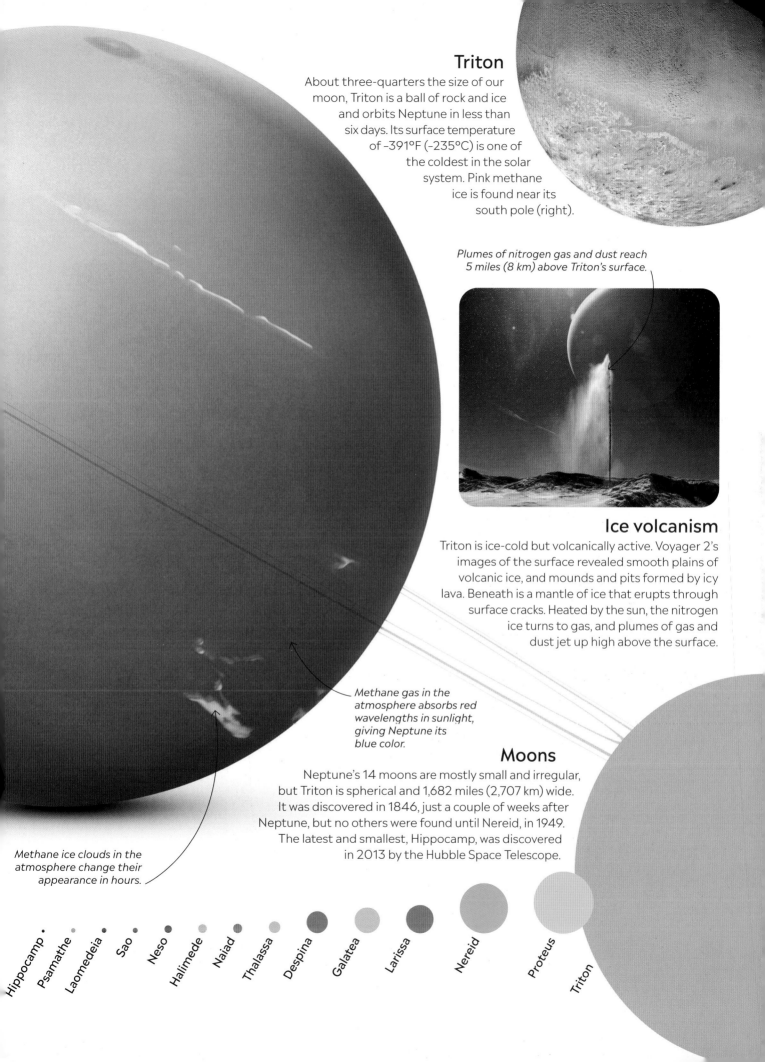

The outer dwarfs

Four known dwarf planets orbit in the Kuiper Belt. Pluto was discovered in 1930 during the search for a ninth major planet, while the others were found among the Kuiper Belt Objects in the early 2000s. All four are small, cold worlds of ice and rock. New Horizons revealed more detail when it flew by Pluto in 2015.

Seeing Pluto close up

New Horizons' images of Pluto showed mountains as high as Earth's Rockies, and the solar system's largest glacier—the crater-free, central region called Sputnik Planitia. This 620-mile (1,000 km) wide ice plain is constantly renewed as older nitrogen ice is replaced by newer material rising from underneath.

Clyde Tombaugh with his own reflecting telescope in 1928

Discovery

American astronomer Clyde Tombaugh joined the Lowell Observatory in Arizona, in 1929. In a search for the ninth planet (Planet X), he took photos of the same region of sky on different nights and compared the images to identify objects that had moved. In February 1930, he found the object later named Pluto.

Mountains capped with methane snow and ice, in the dark Cthulu Regio

Norgay Montes—ice mountains up to 2.2 miles (3.5 km) high—captured by New Horizons in July 2015

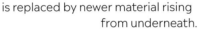

Sputnik Planitia

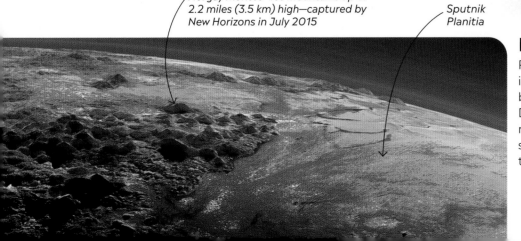

Frozen landscape

Pluto has snowcapped mountain ranges, ice plains, vast canyons, and craters formed by impacts with other Kuiper Belt bodies. During Pluto's 248-year orbit, its thin nitrogen atmosphere freezes to ice and snow and then evaporates again with the changing seasons.

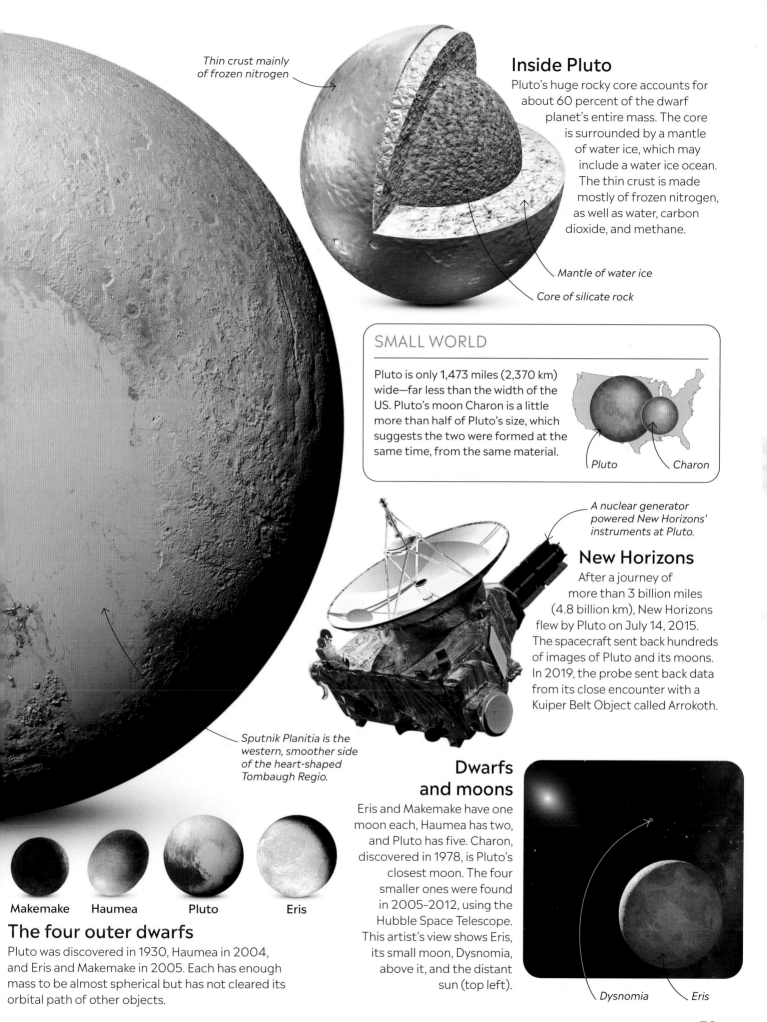

Thin crust mainly of frozen nitrogen

Inside Pluto

Pluto's huge rocky core accounts for about 60 percent of the dwarf planet's entire mass. The core is surrounded by a mantle of water ice, which may include a water ice ocean. The thin crust is made mostly of frozen nitrogen, as well as water, carbon dioxide, and methane.

Mantle of water ice

Core of silicate rock

SMALL WORLD

Pluto is only 1,473 miles (2,370 km) wide—far less than the width of the US. Pluto's moon Charon is a little more than half of Pluto's size, which suggests the two were formed at the same time, from the same material.

Pluto   *Charon*

A nuclear generator powered New Horizons' instruments at Pluto.

New Horizons

After a journey of more than 3 billion miles (4.8 billion km), New Horizons flew by Pluto on July 14, 2015. The spacecraft sent back hundreds of images of Pluto and its moons. In 2019, the probe sent back data from its close encounter with a Kuiper Belt Object called Arrokoth.

Sputnik Planitia is the western, smoother side of the heart-shaped Tombaugh Regio.

Dwarfs and moons

Eris and Makemake have one moon each, Haumea has two, and Pluto has five. Charon, discovered in 1978, is Pluto's closest moon. The four smaller ones were found in 2005–2012, using the Hubble Space Telescope. This artist's view shows Eris, its small moon, Dysnomia, above it, and the distant sun (top left).

Makemake   Haumea   Pluto   Eris

The four outer dwarfs

Pluto was discovered in 1930, Haumea in 2004, and Eris and Makemake in 2005. Each has enough mass to be almost spherical but has not cleared its orbital path of other objects.

Dysnomia   *Eris*

Comets

Visitors from the edge of the solar system, comets are primitive material left over from when the planets formed. These city-sized, dirty snowballs, each on its own orbit around the sun, are mostly too distant to be seen. Every so often, when a star's gravity pushes one much closer to the sun, it becomes a long-tailed comet.

This illustration of a comet nucleus reveals the snow, ice, and rock dust held together loosely by gravity.

Caroline Herschel

German astronomer Caroline Herschel (1750–1848), sister of William Herschel (discoverer of Uranus), was one of the first women to have her work recognized by the scientific community in Europe. She discovered at least five comets.

Dirty snowball nucleus

In the 1950s, American Fred Whipple suggested that the long-tailed comets we see in our skies are produced by a huge, dirty snowball nucleus. In 1986, the Giotto spacecraft imaged the nucleus of Comet Halley. It was a mix of two-thirds snow and ice, one-third rock-dust, 9.5 miles (15.3 km) in length.

The surface loses a layer 3.3 ft (1 m) thick on each close orbit to the sun.

Great comets

About 10 comets a century are bright enough to be easily seen in the night sky and are classed as great comets. Historically, they were named for the year they appeared. Today, they take their discoverer's name. The brightest one so far this century was Comet McNaught in 2007 (above).

Periodic comets

Some comets follow orbits that bring them back time and again to Earth's sky and are called periodic comets. Halley reappears about every 76 years. It shines above the nativity scene in *The Adoration of the Magi* (right), painted by Italian artist Giotto di Bondone in about 1305.

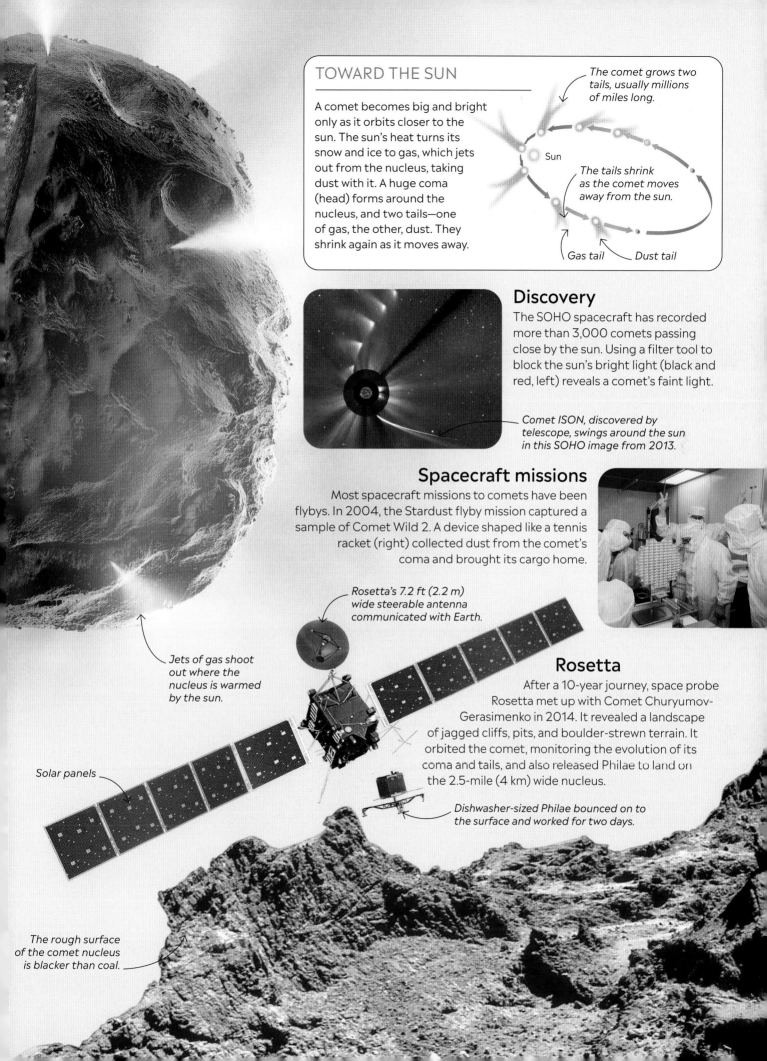

TOWARD THE SUN

A comet becomes big and bright only as it orbits closer to the sun. The sun's heat turns its snow and ice to gas, which jets out from the nucleus, taking dust with it. A huge coma (head) forms around the nucleus, and two tails—one of gas, the other, dust. They shrink again as it moves away.

The comet grows two tails, usually millions of miles long.

Sun

The tails shrink as the comet moves away from the sun.

Gas tail   Dust tail

Discovery

The SOHO spacecraft has recorded more than 3,000 comets passing close by the sun. Using a filter tool to block the sun's bright light (black and red, left) reveals a comet's faint light.

Comet ISON, discovered by telescope, swings around the sun in this SOHO image from 2013.

Spacecraft missions

Most spacecraft missions to comets have been flybys. In 2004, the Stardust flyby mission captured a sample of Comet Wild 2. A device shaped like a tennis racket (right) collected dust from the comet's coma and brought its cargo home.

Rosetta's 7.2 ft (2.2 m) wide steerable antenna communicated with Earth.

Rosetta

After a 10-year journey, space probe Rosetta met up with Comet Churyumov-Gerasimenko in 2014. It revealed a landscape of jagged cliffs, pits, and boulder-strewn terrain. It orbited the comet, monitoring the evolution of its coma and tails, and also released Philae to land on the 2.5-mile (4 km) wide nucleus.

Jets of gas shoot out where the nucleus is warmed by the sun.

Solar panels

Dishwasher-sized Philae bounced on to the surface and worked for two days.

The rough surface of the comet nucleus is blacker than coal.

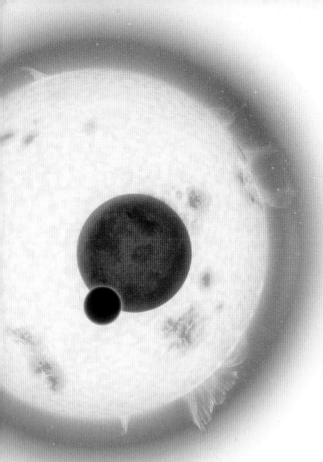

Exoplanets

We know of more than 5,000 planets orbiting other stars. Ranging from near-Earth-like to more massive than Jupiter, exoplanets follow orbits at various distances around different stars. Some orbit as part of a family, but few multiplanet systems resemble our solar system.

Far distant worlds

The known exoplanets orbit about 3,800 stars. In most cases, the star's brightness drowns the light from its planets. The planets can be detected when their gravity causes their star to wobble, or when they pass in front of the star and dim its light. Most exoplanets orbit a single star, but some orbit around a stellar pair. Saturn-sized Kepler-16b (above) orbits a small red star and a larger orange one in 229 days.

Planets around other suns

The first exoplanet found around a sun-like star was 51 Pegasi b, in October 1995. It is massive like Jupiter and hot due to its closeness to its star. It travels around the star 51 Pegasi in just four days. Exoplanets generally take the name of their star, or the name of the spacecraft or project that discovered them, followed by a letter indicating the order of discovery (starting with b).

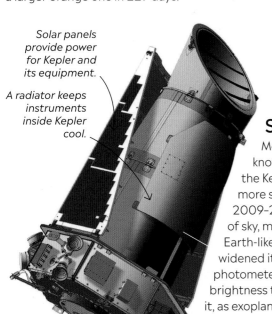

Solar panels provide power for Kepler and its equipment.

A radiator keeps instruments inside Kepler cool.

Thrusters keep the spacecraft in position.

A high-gain antenna transmits data to Earth.

Spacecraft search

More than half the exoplanets known so far were found using the Kepler spacecraft, with many more still awaiting confirmation. In 2009–2013, Kepler studied an area of sky, monitoring 100,000 stars for Earth-like planets, and it later widened its search. Kepler used a photometer that records a star's brightness to spot slight dips in it, as exoplanets pass in front of their parent stars.

👁 EYEWITNESS

Michel Mayor
Swiss astrophysicist Michel Mayor (b.1942) and his colleague Didier Queloz pioneered the discovery of exoplanets in the mid-1990s, thanks to their invention of an advanced spectroscope. The device split starlight into different colors to detect tiny variations caused by their motion as the exoplanets orbited the stars.

This artist's impression depicts Kepler-186f with Earth-like oceans.

Earth-like

The first exoplanets detected were similar in mass to the solar system's giant planets. Less massive ones followed—super-Earths more massive than Earth but not Earth-like in makeup, and now, Earth-like rocky planets. In 2014, Kepler-186f became the first Earth-sized planet to be found in the habitable zone of another star—today, we know of several dozen more. It orbits the star Kepler-186 every 130 days. Four other exoplanets orbit closer to the star and are too hot for water and life to exist.

HR 8799 b

Star HR 8799 is marked by an X—its light has been blocked to reveal the exoplanets.

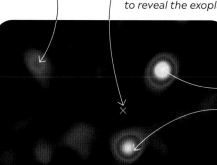

HR 8799 c

HR 8799 d

Family of planets

About 800 stars are known to have multiple planets orbiting them. So far, our own solar system remains one of the largest, tied with Kepler-90 which also has eight planets. Three of the four exoplanets orbiting the star HR 8799 are shown above, in one of the first direct images of a planetary family captured from Earth.

Upsilon Andromedae d

Upsilon Andromedae c

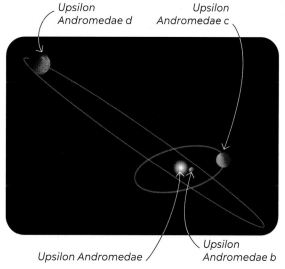

Upsilon Andromedae

Upsilon Andromedae b

Orbits

Some exoplanets are so distant from their star that they take thousands of years to orbit it, while those closer may take just hours or days. Three Jupiter-type exoplanets orbit the star Upsilon Andromedae (left), but two of them—d and c—orbit at unusually steep angles.

Did you **know?**

FASCINATING FACTS

More than 2,000 years ago, Chinese astronomers recorded long-tailed comets sweeping across Earth's night sky. They called them broom stars, or hairy stars.

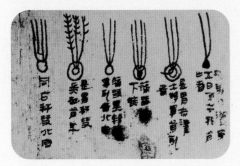

Comets depicted on Mawangdui silk texts (c.300 BCE) from tombs in Hunan, China

Some 19th-century astronomers thought a planet they named Vulcan existed between the sun and Mercury. Vulcan exists only in the science-fiction TV and film series *Star Trek*, as a planet orbiting a distant star.

A new mineral—armalcolite—was found on the moon in July 1969. It takes its name from the three Apollo 11 astronauts, Neil Armstrong, Buzz Aldrin, and Michael Collins.

Personal objects left by astronauts on the moon include two golf balls left behind by Apollo 14's Alan Shepard in 1971, and a family photo placed there in 1972 by Charles Duke, the Apollo 16 astronaut and 10th man to walk on the moon.

On August 5, 2013, one year after Curiosity's arrival on Mars, the rover sang "Happy Birthday" to itself. Technicians on Earth had programmed one of its soil-analysis instruments to vibrate and play the song.

More than 330 meteorites found on Earth are rocks from Mars. They were blasted off the Red Planet when asteroids crashed into it and then followed orbits that brought them to Earth.

In 2014, astronomers discovered that the asteroid Chariklo has two dense, narrow rings—the first found other than the rings around the four giant planets. Chariklo is only 155 miles (250 km) wide and orbits the sun between Saturn and Uranus.

Three toy LEGO® figures 1.5 in (3.8 cm) tall are on board the Juno spacecraft at Jupiter—the Roman god Jupiter, his wife Juno, and the astronomer Galileo Galilei.

The planet Uranus was discovered in 1781, but it may have been seen by the Greek astronomer Hipparchus in 128 BCE. He thought it was a star, as did England's Astronomer Royal, John Flamsteed, when he saw it in 1712.

If you traveled to Neptune—the most distant planet in the solar system—at 62 mph (100 km/h), it would take you 500 years to get there.

The Greek astronomer Hipparchus observing the stars

A 1991 US postage stamp showing Pluto has traveled farther than any other stamp is aboard the New Horizons spacecraft, which flew by Pluto in July 2015.

Historically, comets were seen as bad omens. When Halley's Comet passed by in 1910, Earth moved through its tail. Fearing it was poisonous, some people bought gas masks and anti-comet pills.

Images taken by the Opportunity rover after landing on Mars show what looks like a rabbit. Scientists concluded it was a piece of an airbag used to soften Opportunity's landing, or something similar.

The bunny on Mars

The Opportunity rover, working on Mars since January 2004

QUESTIONS AND ANSWERS

Who names newly discovered planets and moons?

Since the 1920s, the IAU (International Astronomical Union) has overseen the naming of space objects and their features, such as craters, mountains, and maria. Anyone can suggest a name to the IAU, but there are guidelines for each type of object. Dwarf planets, for example, are given the name of a god related to creation. Moons of Jupiter are named after the lovers and descendants of Jupiter, or his Greek equivalent, Zeus.

Who was the last astronaut on the moon?

The last mission to take astronauts to the moon was Apollo 17 in December 1972. Two of its crew, Harrison Schmitt and Eugene Cernan, made three excursions together on to the moon's surface. On the final trip, Cernan led the way out of the landing craft, making Schmitt the last man to step on to the moon. A little over seven hours later, Schmitt was the first back into the craft, making Cernan the last to step off the moon.

Harrison Schmitt collecting samples with a lunar rake

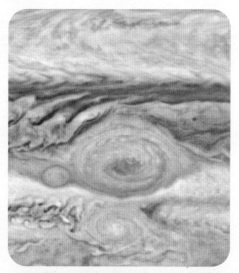

Jupiter's Great Red Spot (center), with Red Spot Jr. (below) and Baby Spot (left), June 2008

Does Jupiter have more than one red spot?

The Great Red Spot is the huge, long-running storm that rages in Jupiter's southern hemisphere. Less well known are its short-lived, smaller companions. Red Spot Jr. first appeared in early 2006 and moved across Jupiter's face below the Great Red Spot. A smaller spot—Baby Red Spot— appeared in 2008 but could not pass unscathed and was quickly consumed by the Great Red Spot.

Has Earth always spun around in 24 hours?

Earth spun about four times faster when it was younger. Friction produced by both the moon and sun's tidal effect on Earth is slowing our planet's spin and moving the Moon away. Currently the Moon moves away by about 3.8 cm (1.5 in) each year. When dinosaurs roamed, Earth's spin was about 21 hours long.

Which is the nearest exoplanet to Earth?

Proxima Centauri b orbits the closest star to the sun, Proxima Centauri, about a quarter of a million times farther from the sun than Earth. A little more massive than Earth, the exoplanet orbits its star every 11 days, within its habitable zone.

How long does it take to send a message to a spacecraft?

The farther a spacecraft travels, the longer it takes to communicate with Earth. Messages to and from rovers on Mars take 14 minutes each way. Voyager 1's signals take 21.6 hours to reach us from interstellar space.

What is the largest telescope on Earth?

The Gran Telescopio Canarias on La Palma in the Canaries, Spain, has the largest mirror, 34.1 ft (10.4 m) across. The Extremely Large Telescope being built in Chile will have a 129 ft (39.3 m) wide mirror.

Dome housing the Gran Telescopio Canarias at La Palma's observatory

RECORD BREAKERS

Longest spin
Venus has the longest spin of any planet, rotating once in 243 days. Massive Jupiter has the shortest, spinning around once in 9.9 hours. Jupiter makes 589 spins during the time it takes Venus to make one.

Slowest orbiter
The more distant a planet is from the sun, the more slowly it orbits. Neptune is the farthest and slowest of the planets. It travels along its orbit at 3.4 miles/s (5.4 km/s). Closest to the sun, Mercury is the fastest, speeding along at 29.5 miles/s (47.4 km/s).

Greatest gravitational pull
The more massive a planet, the greater its gravitational pull. Jupiter's is the greatest, at 2.4 times Earth's. If a rocket could launch from Jupiter, it would need to travel at 36.9 miles/s (59.5 km/s) to escape the planet's gravity.

Solar system **facts**

The eight planets form two groups. Smallest and closest to the sun are the rocky planets Mercury, Venus, Earth, Mars, and just three moons. Farther out and much colder, Jupiter, Saturn, Uranus, and Neptune have faster spins, longer orbits, and numerous moons.

SUN DATA

Diameter	865,374 miles (1,393,684 km)
Mass (Earth = 1)	333,000
Energy output	385 million billion gigawatts
Surface temperature	10,000°F (5,500°C)
Core temperature	27 million°F (15 million°C)
Average distance from Earth	92.9 million miles (149.6 million km)
Rotation period	25 days at the equator

PLANETARY DATA

	Mercury	Venus	Earth	Mars	Jupiter	Saturn	Uranus	Neptune
Diameter in miles (km)	3,032 (4,879)	7,521 (12,104)	7,926 (12,756)	4,220 (6,792)	88,846 (142,984)	74,898 (120,536)	31,763 (51,118)	30,775 (49,528)
Mass (Earth = 1)	0.06	0.82	1	0.11	317.83	95.16	14.54	17.15
Gravity (Earth = 1)	0.38	0.91	1	0.38	2.36	0.92	0.89	1.12
Rotation period in hours	1,407.6	5,832.5	23.9	24.6	9.9	10.7	17.2	16.1
Solar day (sunrise to sunrise) in hours	4,222.6	2,802	24	24.7	9.9	10.7	17.2	16.1
Average temperature	333°F (167°C)	867°F (464°C)	59°F (15°C)	–81°F (–63°C)	–162°F (–108°C)	–218°F (–139°C)	–323°F (–197°C)	–328°F (–201°C)
Closest distance to the sun in miles (km)	28.6 million (46.0 million)	66.8 million (107.5 million)	91.4 million (147.1 million)	128.4 million (206.6 million)	460.1 million (740.5 million)	840.5 million (1,352.6 million)	1,703.4 million (2,741.3 million)	2,761.7 million (4,444.5 million)
Farthest distance from the sun in miles (km)	43.4 million (69.8 million)	67.7 million (108.9 million)	94.5 million (152.1 million)	154.8 million (249.2 million)	507.4 million (816.6 million)	941.1 million (1,514.5 million)	1,866.4 million (3,003.6 million)	2,824.6 million (4,545.7 million)
Orbital period in days	87.96	224.70	365.24	686.97	4,330.59 (11.86 years)	10,746.94 (29.46 years)	30,588.74 (84.01 years)	59,799.9 (164.79 years)
Orbital speed in miles/s (km/s)	29.5 (47.4)	21.7 (35.0)	18.5 (29.8)	14.9 (24.1)	8.1 (13.1)	6.0 (9.7)	4.2 (6.8)	3.4 (5.4)
Number of moons	0	0	1	2	80	83	27	14

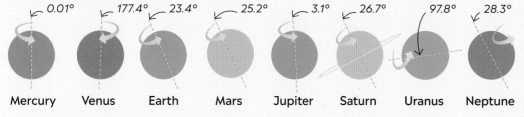

0.01°	177.4°	23.4°	25.2°	3.1°	26.7°	97.8°	28.3°
Mercury	Venus	Earth	Mars	Jupiter	Saturn	Uranus	Neptune

Spin and tilt

All planets spin on an axis (see dotted lines), tilted at an angle. Mercury is the most upright. Venus tilts so far that it spins in the opposite direction. The time taken for one spin (rotation period) is shown in the table above—Earth takes 23.9 hours per spin, but the four giant planets take less.

How far?

The vast distances between the sun and the planets are described using the astronomical unit (au). One au is based on Earth's average distance from the sun.

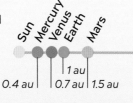

Sun · Mercury · Venus · Earth · Mars

0.4 au | 0.7 au | 1 au | 1.5 au

Jupiter 5.2 au

Saturn 9.5 au

WHAT DO YOU WEIGH?

Apollo 16's John Young on the moon in 1972

Location	% of weight on Earth
Mercury	37.7
Venus	90.8
Earth	100
Moon	16.5
Mars	38.1
Jupiter	236
Saturn	92
Uranus	89
Neptune	112

If you visited other planets, or the moon, your mass (the amount of material you are made of) would stay the same. But your weight is determined by the pull of gravity on mass, and each planet has a different gravitational pull. The greater the pull, the greater your weight. To find your weight on another planet or the moon, multiply your Earth weight by the percentage shown in the table above, and divide the answer by 100.

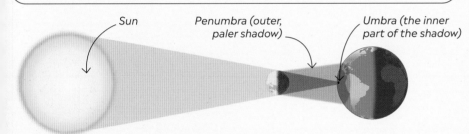

Sun — Penumbra (outer, paler shadow) — Umbra (the inner part of the shadow)

What is a solar eclipse?

The sun is 400 times larger than the moon but 400 times more distant, so they appear the same size in our sky. When the sun, moon, and Earth are directly aligned (above), the sun is eclipsed and hidden from view. The shadow cast by the moon falls on Earth. In the darkest part, or umbra, darkness falls and a total solar eclipse is seen. Anyone in the penumbra (the rest of the shadow) sees a partial eclipse.

VIEW A TOTAL SOLAR ECLIPSE

Date	Visible from this location
04/08/24	Mexico, central US, east Canada
08/12/26	Arctic, Greenland, Iceland, Spain
08/02/27	Spain, north Africa, Saudi Arabia, Yemen
07/22/28	Australia, New Zealand
11/25/30	Botswana, South Africa, Australia
03/30/33	Eastern Russia, Alaska
03/20/34	Central and north Africa, Middle East, Pakistan, China

Key au: astronomical unit
1 au = 92.9 million miles (149.6 million km)

USEFUL WEBSITES

- For all types of NASA space missions—past, present, and future—look at **www.jpl.nasa.gov/missions**
- Follow Perseverance as it roves across Mars, on **mars.nasa.gov/mars2020** and receive its tweets on **twitter.com/NASAMars**
- Find out the latest news on NASA's search for exoplanets and life in other solar systems at **exoplanets.nasa.gov**
- Play games and learn more about space on **www.nasa.gov/kidsclub/index.html** and **www.esa.int/esaKIDSen**

PLACES TO VISIT

VISIT A SPACE CENTER
- At the Kennedy Space Center, Florida, see the rockets that launched astronauts into space, and much more. *www.kennedyspacecenter.com*

VISIT A MUSEUM
- The National Space Centre, Leicester, UK, is packed with interactive galleries, a Rocket Tower, and a planetarium. *spacecentre.co.uk*
- The Herschel Museum of Astronomy, Bath, UK, was William Herschel's home when he discovered Uranus in 1891. *herschelmuseum.org.uk*
- The Cité de l'espace, Toulouse, France, is a theme park dedicated to space. *en.cite-espace.com/discover-the-cite-de-lespace*

VISIT AN OBSERVATORY
- Palomar Observatory, California, is home to the 200-in (5 m) Hale telescope. *www.astro.caltech.edu/palomar/visitor*

VISIT AN IMPACT CRATER
- Walk around the rim and peer deep inside the Barringer Meteorite Crater, Arizona. *www.barringercrater.com*
- See Earth's second-largest impact crater at Wolfe Creek, Western Australia. *parks.dpaw.wa.gov.au/park/wolfe-creek-crater*

Uranus
19 au

Neptune
30 au

Timeline

Earth's sky is our window on the solar system. Our earliest ancestors followed the motions of the sun, moon, and planets. Later, with telescopes, people saw the details on these objects and discovered many more. Spacecraft then became our eyes and laboratories in space, opening up these far-off worlds.

4000 BCE   **500** BCE

Nebra sky disc, Germany, c.1600 BCE

550 BCE Greek mathematician Pythagoras says the sun, moon, Earth, and planets are spherical, not flat.

Pythagoras

4000 BCE Ancient cultures in the Near East use the sun and moon for time keeping, and think five planets—Mercury, Venus, Mars, Jupiter, and Saturn—orbit Earth.

1900

1957 The first spacecraft, Sputnik 1, is put into orbit around Earth by the Soviet Union.

Model of Sputnik 1

1930 American astronomer Clyde Tombaugh discovers a ninth planet—Pluto. Its status is changed to that of dwarf planet in 2006.

1801 Ceres is the first asteroid to be found, by Italy's Giuseppe Piazzi. It is also a dwarf planet.

Yuri Gagarin, inside Vostok 1

1961 Soviet cosmonaut Yuri Gagarin becomes the first human in space, orbiting Earth in Vostok 1.

1959 The Soviet Union's Luna 2 is the first to land on the moon.

1846 German astronomer Johann Galle discovers Neptune, very close to the position predicted by French mathematician Urbain Le Verrier.

Ceres

1960

1962 American spacecraft Mariner 2 makes the first successful flyby of a planet, Venus. Mariner 4 is the first to fly by Mars, in 1965.

1971 Mariner 9 is the first craft to orbit a planet other than Earth. It orbits Mars for almost one year.

1979 The first flyby of Saturn is made by Pioneer 11.

1986 American craft Voyager 2 becomes the first and only craft to fly by Uranus. In 1989, it becomes the only spacecraft to fly by Neptune.

Neil Armstrong on the Moon, 1969

1973 American craft Pioneer 10 is the first to fly by Jupiter. In 1974, Mariner 10 makes the first flyby of Mercury.

1976 The first craft to land on Mars is America's Viking 1, which looks for signs of life.

1969 On July 21, American astronaut Neil Armstrong steps on to the moon, becoming the first human to walk on another world.

1970 The first rover to land on another world, the Soviet Union's Lunokhod 1 explores the moon for 10 months.

1975 The Soviet Union's Venera 9 transmits the first images from the surface of Venus.

Pioneer 11 image of Saturn

1200 CE — 1500 — 1600

1252 The Alphonsine Tables produced by scholars for Alfonso X of Castile list the accurate positions of the sun, moon, and planets for specific dates.

964 CE Persian scholar Abd al-Rahman al-Sufi updates the astronomy of ancient Greece in his *Book of the Fixed Stars*.

1424 Islamic astronomer Ulugh Beg builds his observatory at Samarkand (now in Uzbekistan).

Persian depiction of the Perseus constellation, from the *Book of the Fixed Stars*

Nicolaus Copernicus

1596 The last great naked-eye astronomer, Danish Tycho Brahe completes 20 years of observations. German mathematician Johannes Kepler uses them to form his three laws of planetary motion in 1609–1619.

1543 Polish astronomer Nicolaus Copernicus suggests that the sun is at the center of the universe, orbited by Earth and the other planets.

1800 — 1700 — 1600

Replica of Herschel's telescope

1781 German-born English astronomer William Herschel discovers a new planet—Uranus—doubling the known extent of the solar system.

1687 English scientist Isaac Newton's theory of gravity is published. It explains why the moon orbits Earth and the planets orbit the sun.

Halley's Comet, 1986

1655 Dutch scientist Christiaan Huygens observes Saturn and says it is encircled by a ring. In 1659, he measures the spin period of Mars.

1682 English scientist Edmond Halley sees a comet, calculates its orbit, and predicts its return. Named after him, it returns every 76 years.

1609 The newly invented telescope is used by Italian astronomer Galileo Galilei to study the moon, planets, and stars. In 1610, he publishes his discoveries.

Galileo Galilei

1990 — 2000 — 2020

1992 The first Kuiper Belt object—1992 QB1—is discovered by English astronomer David Jewitt and Vietnamese American astronomer Jane Luu.

51 Pegasi b

1995 The first exoplanet orbiting a sun-like star is detected—51 Pegasi b.

1991 Gaspra is the first asteroid encountered by a spacecraft when the American mission Galileo flies by en route to Jupiter.

2006 Pluto and Eris are reclassified as dwarf planets.

2012 The American rover Curiosity lands on Mars and studies whether Mars could have supported life in the past.

2014 The European Space Agency's Rosetta orbits a comet and releases Philae, the first craft to land on a comet nucleus.

2021 America's Perseverance and China's Zhurong rovers land successfully and begin exploring Mars.

2021 NASA's giant James Webb Space Telescope (JWST), is launched.

2016 Juno, an American spacecraft, becomes the second craft to orbit Jupiter and returns its first images from the planet.

2015 American craft New Horizons flies by Pluto before it heads to Kuiper Belt object Arrokoth.

Juno spacecraft

69

Glossary

ANTENNA An aerial in the shape of a rod, dish, or array for receiving or sending radio signals.

ASTEROID A small rocky body orbiting the sun. Most asteroids are in the Asteroid Belt, between Mars and Jupiter.

ASTEROID BELT A region in the solar system, between the orbits of Mars and Jupiter, that contains a large number of orbiting asteroids.

ASTRONOMICAL UNIT (AU) A unit of length used in astronomy that is equal to about 92.9 million miles (149.6 million km)—Earth's average distance from the sun.

ATMOSPHERE The layer of gases held around a planet, moon, or star by its gravity.

Northern Lights (Aurora Borealis) over a lagoon in Iceland

AURORA A colorful light display above a planet's polar regions—such as Earth's Northern and Southern Lights—produced when electrically charged particles hit atoms in the planet's atmosphere and make them glow.

AXIS The imaginary line that passes through the center of a space object, such as a planet or star, and around which the object rotates, or spins.

BILLION One thousand million (1 followed by nine zeros).

COMET A small body made of snow, ice, and rock dust (called the nucleus). Comets that get deflected from their orbits in the outer solar system and travel near the sun develop a large cloud of gas and dust (the coma) and gas and dust tails.

CORE The innermost region of a planet or star.

CRATER A dish-shaped hollow on the surface of a rocky planet, moon, or asteroid. An impact crater is made by an asteroid, meteorite, or comet hitting the surface. A volcanic crater develops as a volcano ejects material.

CRUST The thin, outermost layer of a rocky or icy body, such as a planet, moon, or comet.

DWARF PLANET An almost round body that orbits the sun but does not have enough mass and gravity to clear its neighborhood of other objects.

ECLIPSE The effect observed when two space bodies are aligned so one appears directly behind the other, or one is in the shadow of the other. In a solar eclipse, when the moon passes between Earth and the sun, the sun is behind the moon in the sky. In a lunar eclipse, the moon passes behind Earth, through Earth's shadow.

EQUATOR The imaginary line drawn around the middle of a planet, moon, or star, halfway between its north and south poles, separating its northern and southern hemispheres.

EXOPLANET A planet that orbits around a star other than the sun.

FLYBY A close encounter made with a solar system object by a spacecraft that flies past without going into orbit.

GALAXY An enormous grouping of stars, gas, and dust held together by gravity. The sun is one of the stars in the Milky Way Galaxy.

GAS GIANT A large planet, such as Jupiter or Saturn, that consists mainly of hydrogen and helium, which are in gaseous form at the planet's visible surface.

GIANT PLANET Any planet that is large and massive compared with Earth. In the solar system, the four biggest planets—Jupiter, Saturn, Uranus, and Neptune—are classed as giant planets.

GRAVITY A force of attraction found throughout the universe. The greater the mass of a body, the greater its gravitational pull.

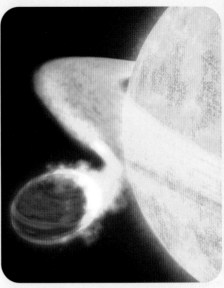

The doomed hot Jupiter WASP-12b is being eaten by its parent star

HABITABLE Suitable for living in or on. Life may exist on a planet that orbits within the habitable zone around a star.

HEMISPHERE One-half of a sphere. Earth is divided into northern and southern hemispheres by its equator.

HOT JUPITER A type of exoplanet that is more massive than Jupiter but orbits closer to its star than Mercury to the sun.

ICE GIANT A giant planet composed mainly of elements heavier than hydrogen and helium. The solar system's two ice giants are Uranus and Neptune.

INNER PLANETS The planets nearest the sun in the solar system—Mercury, Venus, Earth, and Mars.

INTERSTELLAR SPACE The region between the stars in a galaxy—in the solar system, it is the space beyond the planets.

Apollo 11's lunar module, Eagle—the first lander to put people on the moon

KUIPER BELT OBJECT (KBO)
A rock-and-ice body orbiting the sun in the Kuiper Belt, beyond Neptune's orbit.

LANDER A spacecraft that lands on the surface of a planet, moon, asteroid, or comet.

LUNAR Relating to the moon, such as a lunar module built to land on the moon.

MAGNETIC FIELD
The region around a magnetized body, where magnetic forces affect the motion of electrically charged particles. Earth's magnetic field, for example, is generated by flows in the planet's liquid outer core.

MANTLE A thick layer of rock between the core and the crust of a planet or moon.

MASS A measure of how much matter (material) a body is made of.

METEOR A short-lived streak of light—also called a shooting star—produced by a tiny, grain-sized piece of comet or asteroid speeding through Earth's upper atmosphere.

METEORITE A piece of rock or metal that lands on the surface of a planet or moon and survives the impact; most are pieces of asteroid.

MILKY WAY The spiral-shaped galaxy that includes the sun and about 200 billion other stars. Also the stars visible to the naked eye as a band of faint light across the night sky.

MOON A rock or rock-and-ice body that orbits a planet, dwarf planet, or asteroid.

NUCLEAR FUSION A process in which atomic nuclei join to form heavier nuclei and release huge amounts of energy such as heat and light. In the sun's core, hydrogen nuclei fuse to produce helium.

NUCLEUS (PLURAL NUCLEI) The compact central core of an atom. Also the solid, icy body of a comet.

OORT CLOUD The sphere consisting of billions of comets that surrounds the planetary part of the solar system.

ORBIT The path of a natural or artificial object around another more massive body, influenced by its gravity.

ORBITER A spacecraft that orbits a space body such as a planet, moon, or asteroid.

Incoming meteorite

OUTER PLANETS The four planets that orbit the sun beyond the Asteroid Belt – Jupiter, Saturn, Uranus, and Neptune.

PARTICLE An extremely small part of a solid, liquid, or gas.

PHASE The part of a moon or planet that is lit by the sun and visible from Earth. The moon passes through a cycle of phases every 29.5 days.

PLANE A flat, two-dimensional area. In the solar system, the planets travel around the sun at different distances but close to the same orbital plane.

PLANET A massive, nearly round body that orbits the sun and shines by reflecting the star's light.

PROBE An unmanned spacecraft built to explore objects in space—particularly their atmosphere and surface—and transmit information back to Earth.

ROCKY PLANET A planet composed mainly of rock, such as the four planets closest to the sun – Mercury, Venus, Earth, and Mars.

ROVER A vehicle driven remotely on a planet or moon.

SATELLITE An artificial object that is deliberately placed in orbit around Earth or another solar system body. Also a natural object such as a moon or any space object orbiting another, more massive body.

SHEPHERD MOON
A small moon whose gravitational pull herds orbiting particles into a well-defined ring around a planet.

SOFT LANDING
A controlled landing by a vehicle, including a spacecraft. A hard landing may result in the craft being destroyed, intentionally or accidentally.

SOLAR Relating to the sun.

SOLAR SYSTEM The sun and all the objects orbiting it, such as the planets and many smaller bodies.

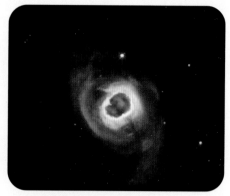

Dying star, a glimpse of our sun's future

STAR A huge, spinning sphere of very hot, luminous gas that generates energy by nuclear fusion in its core. The sun is a star.

SUPER-EARTH A type of exoplanet with a mass greater than Earth but smaller than the ice giants Uranus and Neptune.

TELESCOPE An instrument that uses lenses or mirrors, or a combination of the two, to collect and focus light to form a magnified image of a distant object. Some telescopes collect other wavelengths besides visible light, such as radio and infrared.

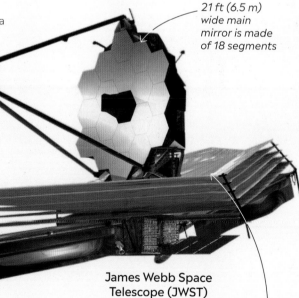

21 ft (6.5 m) wide main mirror is made of 18 segments

James Webb Space Telescope (JWST)

The sunshield protects the JWST from sunlight, cooling it to less than -370°F (-223°C).

UNIVERSE Everything that exists—all space and everything in it.

VOLCANISM The eruption of molten rock on to the surface of a planet or moon through volcanic vents, often resulting in extensive flows of lava.

Index

AB

Aldrin, Buzz 14, 30
animals 26, 27
Apollo 11 spacecraft 14, 30–31
Armstrong, Neil 14, 30
Asteroid Belt 38, 39
asteroids 18, 28, 29, 33
  exploring 38–39, 43
  the moon 31
  solar system 7
astronauts 14, 23, 30–31
astronomers 9, 13, 43, 48, 50, 52, 53, 60
  see also Galilei, Galileo
atmospheres 10
  Earth 11, 22
  Jupiter 40–41
  Mars 34
  Saturn 45
  Venus 18
auroras 40
BepiColombo probe 19

CD

canyons 32, 34, 35, 55, 58
carbohydrates 16
carbon dioxide 18, 59
Carruthers, George 29
Cassini, Giovanni 46
Cassini spacecraft 50, 51
China 30, 37
Collins, Michael 30
comets 7, 40, 60–61
Copernicus, Nicolaus 12
craters 10, 18, 32, 35, 39, 58
  see also volcanoes
Curiosity ChemCam 36, 37
Darwin, Charles 27
dwarf planets 7, 8, 38, 52, 53, 58–59

EF

Earth 8, 12
  asteroids, and 39
atmosphere 11, 22
ever-changing surface 23
the moon 7
orbit, spin, and seasons 22
solar system 6
view from space 22–23
volcanoes 10
water 24–25
eclipses 17, 29, 67
Eris 7, 8
erosion 11
European ExoMars 37
exoplanets 8, 9, 62–63
extinction 27
extremophiles 27
fungi 26

GH

galaxies 9, 13
Galilean moons, 42–43
Galilei, Galileo 12, 30, 42, 44
Galileo spacecraft 50
giant planets 6, 10, 50–51
gravity 31, 40, 42
  and rings 46–47
  and tides 24
greenhouse effect 21
Halley, Edmond and
  Halley's Comet 60, 69
helium 40–41, 55
Herschel, Caroline 60
Herschel, William 52
Hubble Space Telescope 56, 57
human population 26
Huygens, Christiaan 44, 48
Huygens probe 49, 51
hydrogen 6, 17, 40–41, 44, 55
Hyperion (moon) 48

IJK

ice 25, 33, 35, 58
International

Astronomical Union (IAU) 8
Jemison, Mae 14
Juno spacecraft 15, 42, 50, 51, 64
Jupiter 6
  atmosphere 40–41
  exploring 50, 51
  Great Red Spot 10
  mass 13
  moons 7, 42–43
Kepler, Johannes 13, 62
Kepler spacecraft 62
Kepler-186f 63
Kuiper Belt 52, 53, 58

L

Leavitt, Henrietta 13
life
  on Earth 22
  human impact on 26
  kingdoms and species 26
  search for life elsewhere 27
Luna spacecraft 14, 30, 31

M

magnetism 19, 40, 51
Mariner spacecraft 14, 19
Mars 32–37
  craters 35
  exploring 12, 14, 15, 36–37
  liquid water 11
  moons 7, 33
Mayor, Michel 62
Mercury 7, 8, 18–19
  exploring 14
  rocky surface 11, 18, 19
  view from Earth 18
Messenger spacecraft 19
meteorites 38, 39
methane 49, 55, 56, 59
microorganisms 26, 27
Milky Way Galaxy 9
monerans and protists 26
moon, Earth's 7, 28–29
  eclipses 29
  exploring 14, 30–31

gravity 24
orbit and rotation 28–29
phases 29, 30
moons
  dwarf planets 59
  Jupiter 42–43
  Mars 7, 33
  Neptune 56–57
  Saturn 48–49
  Uranus 54, 55
Morabito, Linda 43
mountains 25, 29, 30, 58

NO

NASA 14, 15, 50
Neptune 6, 9, 52, 56–57
  atmosphere 56
  exploring 50
  moons 56–57
  view from Earth 7
New Horizons probe 52, 59
nitrogen 22, 59
nuclear fusion 16
observatories 13
oceans, Earth 11, 22, 24, 25
Oort Cloud 52, 53
orbits 6, 7, 8, 28–29
  see also rotation;
  individual names of planets
oxygen 16, 22
ozone layer 22

PQR

Parker Solar Probe 17
Payne-Gaposchkin, Cecilia 17
photosynthesis 16
Piccard, Jacques 24
Pioneer spacecraft 50
planets
  defining, and naming of 8–9
  dwarf and exoplanets 8
  masses 13
  solar system 6–7
plants 26
Pluto 7, 8, 52, 53, 58–59

protists and monerans 26
Queloz, Didier 62
rings 41, 46–47, 55, 56
rivers 24, 32
robotic spacecraft
  see spacecraft
rocky planets 10–11
Rosetta spacecraft 61
rotation (spin) 29, 40, 54, 66

S

Sagan, Carl 50
sand dunes 35
satellites 17, 22, 25
Saturn 6, 44–49
  atmosphere 45
  early observations 44
  exploring 50, 51
  moons 7, 48–49
  rings 44, 46–47
Schweickart, Russell Louis 23
seasons 7, 22, 32, 56, 58
Sedna 7, 53
solar eclipse 17, 67
solar system 7, 12, 52–53
Soviet Union 14, 30–31
spacecraft
  exploring asteroids 39
  exploring comets 60, 61
  exploring Mars 27
  exploring Mercury 19
  exploring the moon 14–15
  exploring Neptune 56
  exploring the outer planets 50–51, 59
  exploring Venus 20, 21
stars 13, 62–63
  see also Sun
Stonehenge 12
storms 10, 17, 40, 41, 45, 56
sun
  ancient peoples' observations 12
  and comets 61
  energy from 16
  mass 6, 16

studying the 17, 35

T

tectonic plates 23
telescopes 12, 13, 27, 30, 57
tides 24
Titan (moon) 48–49, 51
Tombaugh, Clyde 58
Triton (moon) 57
Trujillo, Diana 37

U

United States of America 15, 27, 30–31
Uranus 6, 9, 52, 54–55
  exploring 50
  moons 54, 55
  orbit and rotation 54
  view from Earth 7

V

Venera spacecraft 15, 20
Venus 7, 9
  atmosphere 11, 20
  exploring 14
  rocky surface 21
  spacecraft 15
Vesta 38
Viking spacecraft 33
volcanoes 10, 19
  Earth 25
  Jupiter 43
  Mars 32, 34
  the moon 29, 31
  Venus 21
Voyager spacecraft 41, 43, 50–51, 54, 55, 56–57

W

water
  on Earth 11, 24–25
  on Mars 32
  on Neptune 56
  on Pluto 59
  on Uranus 55
Whipple, Fred 60
winds 17, 40, 41, 45

Acknowledgments

Dorling Kindersley would like to thank:
Ann Baggaley for proofreading, Ashok Kumar and Rakesh Kumar for DTP assistance, and Vishal Ghavri and Deepak Negi for picture research assistance.

The publisher would like to thank the following for their kind permission to reproduce their photographs:

(Key: a-above; b-below/bottom; c-centre; f-far; l-left; r-right; t-top)

123RF.com: ammit 10br; **Alamy Stock Photo:** dpa picture alliance archive 39bc, Granger Historical Picture Archive 12tr, North Wind Picture Archives 12br, DPA picture alliance 62br, Ann E Parry 23br, GL Archive 13bl, PhotoStock-Israel / Historic Illustrations 48cra, IanDagnall Computing / NASA 14bc, NASA Photo 50bc, BNA Photographic 24cb; **Dorling Kindersley:** Simon Mumford 4-5tc, NASA 43ca; **Dreamstime.com:** Andrey Andronov 69ca, Sean Beckett 27crb, Delstudio 29c, Heisenberg85 26crb, Inge Hogenbijl 65cr, Inigocia 12-13c, Igor Kovalchuk 17bc, Jamen Percy 70clb, Pixattitude 34cbl, Typhoonski 9bl, Oleg Znamenskiy 16crb; ESA: 19br, ATG medialab 61cb, DLR / FU Berlin (G. Neukum) 32br, 35cb, DLR / FU Berlin, CC BY-SA 3.0 IGO 33bl, J. Whatmore 11tr, NASA / JHU Applied Physics Lab / Carnegie Inst. Washington 6clb, 18-19cr, R. Lockwood 33crb, NASA / The Hubble Heritage Team (STScI / AURA) / R. Sahai and J. Trauger (Jet Propulsion Laboratory) 71tr; ESO: Y. Beletsky / http://creativecommons.org/licenses/by/3.0 13cb, 18cl, L. Calçada and Nick Risinger / http://creativecommons.org/licenses/by/3.0 (Eris), http://creativecommons.org/licenses/by/3.0 55c, 60cb, 69c, NASA / Jeff Schmaltz / http://creativecommons.org/licenses/by/3.0 39cr, M. Kornmesser / Nick Risinger (skysurvey.org) http://creativecommons.org/licenses/by/3.0 69cb, D. Schreiner and S. Degezelle / http://creativecommons.org/licenses/by/3.0 29cr; **Getty Images:**

Dea / A. Dagli Orti 60br, Archive Photos 64cra, Bettmann 58cbr, Jonathan Blair 53crb, De Agostini Picture Library 46tr, Dea Picture Library 69cr, Heritage Images / Hulton Fine Art Collection / Landesamt fr Denkmalpflege and Archologie Sachsen-Anhalt 68tc, 69tl, John Russell 52bl, Science & Society Picture Library 69cla, Gail Shumway 26tl, Stocktrek Images 30tl, Thomas J. Abercrombie 39bl, Universal Images Group 25t; Eliot Herman: 7tr; NASA and The Hubble Heritage Team (AURA/STScI): ESA / A. Simon (Goddard Space Flight Center) 10fcrb, ESA / A. Simon-Miller (NASA Goddard Space Flight Center) 65ca, ESA / Adolf Schaller 53bc, ESA / Adolph Schaller (for STScI) 59br, Erich Karkoschka (University of Arizona) 54clb, ESA 43cra, NASA / ESA / A. Simon (Goddard Space Flight Center) 6bl, 40ca, NASA / ESA / J. Nichols (University of Leicester) 40c, ESA / H. Hammel (Space Science Institute and AURA) 10crb, ESA / H. Teplitz and M. Rafelski (IPAC / Caltech) / A. Koekemoer (STScI) / R. Windhorst (Arizona State University) 13cla, ESA / M.H. Wong / J. Tollefson (UC Berkeley) 56bl, ESA / R. Beebe (New Mexico State University) 10cb, ANDREW CABALLERO-REYNOLDS / AFP 9br, Vivien Killilea / Getty Images North America 37br, Print Collector / Hulton Archive 27tc, Bettmann 17bl, Bettmann 55tr; **Getty Images / iStock:** Byelaman 2cr, 36tr; **Library of Congress, Washington, D.C.:** NASA: ESA / A. Feild (STScI) 63bc, 4l, 6clb, 11crb, 14crb, 14tr, 15l, 19tc, 19crb, 20cla, 20bl, 23bc, 24cl, 26bc, 30cb, 30-31b, 31tr, 31cr, 50cbr, 51l, 59clb (Haumea), 61cr, 64cla, 65bl, 67cla, 68cla, 68clb, 68br, GSFC / Arizona State University 30tr, Neil Armstrong 70br, JPL-Caltech / University of Arizona 5tr, 15tc, JPL-Caltech / ASI / Cornell 49tl, JPL-Caltech / Cornell / ASU 10clb, JPL-Caltech / Hap McSween (University of Tennessee), and Andrew Beck and Tim McCoy (Smithsonian Institution) 2cl, 38cr, JPL-Caltech / Keck 47cb, JPL-Caltech / KSC 42tr, JPL-Caltech / LANL / J.-L. Lacour, CEA 37cbl, JPL-Caltech / MSSS 15ca, 34-35c, 37tl, JPL-Caltech / Palomar Observatory 63clb, JPL-Caltech / Space Science Institute 45tr, 45bc, 48tr, JPL-Caltech / SSI / Hampton University 4crb,

45crb, JPL-Caltech / UCLA / MPS / DLR / IDA 38t, 68cr, JPL-Caltech / University of Arizona 33tc, 33cla, 33cra, JPL / Cornell 35cr, JPL / Cornell University 64b, JPL / DLR 42-43c, ESA 17tr, 49cl, ESA / G. Bacon 70tr, Aubrey Gemignani 19tc (MESSENGER), Goddard / Arizona State University 29cr, GRIN 50ctr, NSSDC / GSFC 40crb, Johns Hopkins University Applied Physics Laboratory / Carnegie Institution of Washington 9t, 11ca, 19cra, Johns Hopkins University Applied Physics Laboratory / Southwest Research Institute 8cl, 59cb, The Hubble Heritage Team (STScI / AURA) Acknowledgment: R.G. French (Wellesley College), J. Cuzzi (NASA / Ames), L. Dones (SwRI), and J. Lissauer (NASA / Ames) 47tc, R. Hurt (SSC-Caltech) / JPL-Caltech 53clb, JPL 4cra, 15br, 20-21c, 21crb, 25cr, 32-33cs, 35cbl, 41cl, 51ca, 55tc, 55bc, 56cl, 64c, 64-65 (Background), 66-67 (Background), 68-69 (Background), 70-71 (Background), JPL-Caltech 6crb, 28cl, 32l, 36cra, 51crb, 62tl, 62cr, 69br, Ulli Lotzmann 31tl, M. Ahmetvaleev 39t, ESA / Rosetta / NAVCAM 61b, SDO 16l, 17cl, Ames / SETI Institute / JPL-Caltech 63tr, ESA / SOHO 17cr, ESA / SOHO / GSFC 61ca, JPL / Space Science Institute 7crb, 41r, 45tc, 46ca, 47ca, 47cra, 48cr, JHUAPL / SwRI 3c, 53cb, 58bl, 58-59cs, 59clb (Pluto), JPL / USGS 57cr, 4-5t, 71br, 24-25t, JPL-Caltech 25tr, 15c, JPL-Caltech 37bc, NASA / JPL-Caltech / SwRI / MSSS / Jason Major 10bl (year 2017), NOAA 6c, 22-23c, 999Wallchartcra; **Science Photo Library:** NASA / JPL / ARIZONA STATE UNIVERSITY 34-35t, Detlev Van Ravensway 17crb, Dr Seth Shostak 27bl, Take 27 Ltd 2bl, 10-11c; Copyright © Subaru Telescope, National Astronomical Observatory of Japan (NAOJ). All right reserved.: 43br; Dr Dominic Fortes, UCL: 57cra; Wellcome Images http://creativecommons.org/licenses/by/4.0/: Iconographic Collections 68cra; Wikipedia: 31c, CLAUS LUNAU 21l, 17tc, NASA, ESA, CSA, JUPITER ERS TEAM; JUDY SCHMIDT 2tr, 41cb, PAUL D STEWART 60cl; **Shutterstock.com:** NASA / ZUMA Wire (29br), Uncredited / AP (52crb)

All other images © Dorling Kindersley

WHAT WILL YOU EYEWITNESS NEXT?

Packed with pictures and full of facts, DK Eyewitness books are perfect for school projects and home learning.

  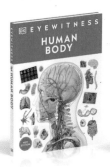   

   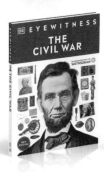  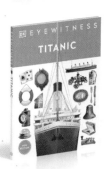

 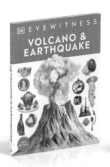  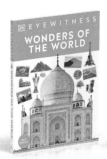 

Also available:

Eyewitness Amphibian
Eyewitness Ancient China
Eyewitness Ancient Civilizations
Eyewitness Ancient Greece
Eyewitness Animal
Eyewitness Arms and Armor
Eyewitness Astronomy
Eyewitness Aztec, Inca & Maya
Eyewitness Baseball
Eyewitness Bible Lands
Eyewitness Bird
Eyewitness Car

Eyewitness Castle
Eyewitness Chemistry
Eyewitness Crystals & Gems
Eyewitness Dog
Eyewitness Early People
Eyewitness Eagle and Birds of Prey
Eyewitness Electricity
Eyewitness Endangered Animals
Eyewitness Energy
Eyewitness Flight
Eyewitness Forensic Science
Eyewitness Fossil
Eyewitness Great Scientists

Eyewitness Horse
Eyewitness Insect
Eyewitness Judaism
Eyewitness Knight
Eyewitness Medieval Life
Eyewitness Mesopotamia
Eyewitness Money
Eyewitness Mummy
Eyewitness Mythology
Eyewitness National Parks
Eyewitness North American Indian
Eyewitness Plant
Eyewitness Prehistoric Life

Eyewitness Presidents
Eyewitness Religion
Eyewitness Reptile
Eyewitness Robot
Eyewitness Shakespeare
Eyewitness Soccer
Eyewitness Soldier
Eyewitness Space Exploration
Eyewitness Tree
Eyewitness Universe
Eyewitness Vietnam War
Eyewitness Viking
Eyewitness World War I

ORCA FOOTPRINTS

Too Much Trash

HOW LITTER IS HURTING ANIMALS

JOAN MARIE GALAT

ORCA BOOK PUBLISHERS

Text copyright © Joan Marie Galat 2023

Published in Canada and the United States in 2023 by Orca Book Publishers.
orcabook.com

Library and Archives Canada Cataloguing in Publication

Title: Too much trash : how litter is hurting animals / Joan Marie Galat.
Names: Galat, Joan Marie, 1963- author. Series: Orca footprints ; 27.
Description: Series statement: Orca footprints ; 27 |
Includes bibliographical references and index.
Identifiers: Canadiana (print) 202202660158 |
Canadiana (ebook) 202202660166 |
ISBN 9781459831827 (hardcover) | ISBN 9781459831834 (PDF) |
ISBN 9781459831841 (EPUB)
Subjects: LCSH: Habitat (Ecology)—Juvenile literature. |
LCSH: Refuse and refuse disposal—Juvenile literature. |
LCSH: Pollution—Juvenile literature. |
LCSH: Human-animal relationships—Juvenile literature. |
LCSH: Nature—Effect of human beings on—Juvenile literature. |
LCSH: Habitat conservation—Juvenile literature.
Classification: LCC QH75 .G35 2023 | DDC j591.72/7—dc23

Library of Congress Control Number: 2022938871

Summary: Part of the nonfiction Orca Footprints series for middle-
grade readers, this book examines how garbage hurts animals and
their habitats. Illustrated with photographs throughout.

Orca Book Publishers is committed to reducing the consumption of
nonrenewable resources in the production of our books. We make
every effort to use materials that support a sustainable future.

Orca Book Publishers gratefully acknowledges the support
for its publishing programs provided by the following
agencies: the Government of Canada, the Canada Council for
the Arts and the Province of British Columbia through the
BC Arts Council and the Book Publishing Tax Credit.

Front cover images by zanskar/Getty Images and Visionhaus/Getty Images.
Back cover images by Milos Momcilovic/Shutterstock.com,
Stock-Asso/Shutterstock.com and Ian Dyball/Getty Images.

Design by Jenn Playford
Edited by Kirstie Hudson

Printed and bound in South Korea.

26 25 24 23 • 1 2 3 4

*Lost or abandoned fishing nets, called ghost nets,
can still trap animals. Littered nets endanger
the lives of aquatic species like this seal.*
IAN DYBALL/GETTY IMAGES

For Keller Clarke, who deserves to inhabit a pristine world.

Contents

Introduction 6

CHAPTER ONE
THE TROUBLE WITH LITTER

More Than Ugly 8
Bad Eating Habits 10
Mistakes Animals Make 11
Who's in Charge of Litter? 14
No Mess, No Stress 15

CHAPTER TWO
WHERE LITTER IS BORN

A Look at Litterbugs 16
Guess the Mess 19
Waste Woes 19
Is This Littering? 20
Prevention Is Best 22

CHAPTER THREE
WASTE IN THE WILD

This Habitat Is My Home 24

The Decay Factor 26

How Long Does Marine Debris Last? 27

Pollution: From Land to Sky 28

Put Out the Fire 28

Traveling Trash 29

Sinking Litter 30

Reach Down, Pick Up 31

CHAPTER FOUR
LET'S FIX THIS PROBLEM

People with Plans 34

Sensational Solutions 35

Marvelous Machines 36

Could You Be an Anti-Litter Activist? 37

Cost of Waste 37

Combating Litter 39

A Litter-Free Tomorrow Starts Today 41

Acknowledgments 42

Resources 43

Glossary 44

Index 46

Introduction

One way to reduce littering is to empty trash bins frequently. Increasing the number of containers in busy public places also helps.
LOIS GOBE/SHUTTERSTOCK.COM

When I was 11 years old, I volunteered for the annual Alberta spring highway cleanup. I thought I'd done my share after filling a couple of garbage bags and heaving them into the back of a pickup truck. But it turned out our group was expected to clean several miles of highway. The horrifying amount of trash we found left me wanting to understand why people treat our *environment* this way. I wondered, What does all this litter mean for the animals we share the planet with?

Walking down a street or through a park, you probably notice garbage too. You might dodge a cigarette butt, crumpled tissue or glob of gum. It's foul and germy and unpleasant. It's natural to wonder why people don't just use trash cans.

Most will agree that scattered waste is unsightly. It's more than ugly though. Litter can have a major effect on wildlife, pets and farm animals. Tossed trash often ends up in water. It travels long distances, from rivers to seas, adding waste to our oceans. Animals that get tangled in litter or eat plastics or poisonous objects may become injured or sick. Many die.

What will it take to clean up our planet? Around the world people are trying to answer this question. In this book you'll discover the many ways litter can hurt animals, how people are finding solutions and what you can do to help prevent litter.

Removing gum from pavement and other surfaces is a costly and time-consuming chore. Modern chewing gum creates plastic waste that may last from tens to hundreds of years before breaking down.
AFRICA STUDIO/SHUTTERSTOCK.COM

You can help restore animal habitat by picking up litter. Cleanup campaigns help raise awareness about the consequences of litter and inspire volunteers to reduce their use of plastics. STOCK-ASSO/SHUTTERSTOCK.COM

CHAPTER ONE

The Trouble With Litter

MORE THAN UGLY

Help make your trash less attractive to critters. Rinse off any food waste to reduce smells and cut up any product or material that an animal could get tangled in. Use a sturdy bin to make it hard for animals to access household waste.

JOSHUA RESNICK/SHUTTERSTOCK.COM

Most people throw things away every day. It might be unwanted food, a plastic sandwich bag or a candy wrapper. As a resident of Earth, you make decisions about your stuff all the time. You might give away the clothes you outgrow or sort trash for recycling. Maybe you turn kitchen scraps into *compost*. According to the World Bank, each person creates an average of 1.6 pounds (0.73 kilograms) of waste every day. Some is disposed of safely. It goes into garbage bins or dumpsters, eventually reaching a waste-management facility. Sometimes, though, people drop trash on the ground.

Litter is any unwanted item left where it does not belong. You might see it on sidewalks or twirling in a whirlwind. You might spot trash building up along a fence, dropped in a ditch or floating in a pond. Litter includes apple cores, orange peels and other organic waste, along with disposable cups, plates and utensils. It can be dirty diapers or plastic bags, straws and bottles.

Cigarette butts are the most commonly littered item. Plentiful and deadly, they can take from 2 to 25 years to *decompose*, depending on their exposure to sun, water and other conditions. Even large items like furniture, tires or old appliances are sometimes dumped outdoors. All this refuse gets in the way of animals who need to forage for food and find nesting sites without garbage in their way.

Hopefully, you choose not to be a *litterbug*. Bits of litter add up to tons of garbage over time. When it comes to getting rid of stuff, your choices are important. They can promote *sustainability*. Your decisions can help keep our planet green and clean for the 8.7 million species of animals living here.

Cigarette filters are made from a type of plastic called cellulose acetate. When littered, cigarette butts release plastic, nicotine and other pollutants. Bins like this prevent toxins from leaching into ecosystems and reduce the risk of cigarettes starting garbage-can fires. ALENA VEASEY/SHUTTERSTOCK.COM

Tires contain natural and synthetic rubber as well as chemicals and heavy metals. As tires break down, they release toxins that pollute waterways where aquatic species live. MAURICIO HANDLER/GETTY IMAGES

BAD EATING HABITS

If someone shouts "Free food!" you probably want to check it out. Animals like easy meals too. Critters that see or smell litter want to investigate. Eating discarded food, however, is a habit that can hurt their health. Whether it's a dropped onion ring, piece of bread or meat chunk, our scraps are not harmless. Most human foods are **processed.** The fats, spices, artificial flavors and other ingredients we add to our meals can make animals sick. Components such as salt and sugars attract animals to human food. Just as we do, animals prefer certain tastes. Species that like specific foods will seek them out. Ducks, for example, will leave water to eat bread, popcorn and other picnic litter. Certain fixings can upset animals' digestive systems and leave them without needed **nutrients**. Over time, animals that continue to eat human food will experience serious health problems. Ducks that eat a diet high in proteins and carbohydrates may develop angel wing. This condition causes wing feathers to stick out sideways, preventing flight.

Plentiful litter can lead animals to become **urban exploiters.** An abundance of food rubbish can lead to obesity, as well as overpopulation. When trash attracts many animals to one place, illnesses spread more easily. This can lead to an increase in **zoonotic diseases**. Rodents may breed in places where waste has been dumped and spread sicknesses to people. Flies also carry **germs** they pick up from garbage.

AROUND THE WORLD

Sometimes food litter is in containers or wrapped in plastic, foil or paper. You probably know what it's like to want something that is trapped in packaging. Maybe you've struggled to tease open a bag, but you found a way. An animal doesn't give up either. Its solution can be to swallow the packaging along with the food, which can damage its body, including its mouth, throat, esophagus, intestine or other body parts.

MISTAKES ANIMALS MAKE

Mistaking littered objects for food is another serious problem. Animals may choke after swallowing plastics or latex items like balloons or gloves. Eating garbage can also make them feel full and stop them from seeking out their natural diets, which in turn can lead to **malnutrition**. Animals can starve if swallowed objects block their digestive systems. They also risk poisoning from licking antifreeze, household cleaners or other toxic products.

Litter can lead wild creatures to associate humans with food and lose their natural fear of people, a process called animal **habituation.**

We may use a plastic bag for part of a day, but a littered plastic sack can last in the environment and put animals at risk for years. Plastics commonly contain ingredients designed to make them flexible, strong and long-lasting.
LILLIAN TVEIT/SHUTTERSTOCK.COM

The phrase cunning as a fox *arose because these canines are clever when it comes to finding a meal. Sometimes, though, their ability to locate food leads to deadly encounters with trash.* GELEFIN/SHUTTERSTOCK.COM

Animal-resistant garbage bins only work if their lids are firmly closed. If you're in bear country and the closest container is full, take your trash to another safe-disposal site.
JEFF OLIVIER/SHUTTERSTOCK.COM

It can create conditions that are dangerous for both humans and animals. People might get too close to wildlife that appears tame. Startled animals might bite, kick, claw or use other defenses to protect themselves. If they threaten people or property, they may end up being killed.

Some types of trash harm animals by causing injury and infection. Creatures may cut themselves on littered glass, jagged metal or other sharp objects. They may even get stuck in garbage! Animals seeking food are known to jam their heads or other body parts into jars or cans and get stuck, or climb into plastic bags and suffocate. Those tangled in rope, string or nets may be unable to move. As they grow, young animals caught in plastic six-pack rings can find their necks getting pinched tighter and tighter. Disposable masks, commonly scattered on the ground since the COVID-19 pandemic began in 2019, are becoming tangled around birds' necks, wings and feet. Cats and dogs are just some of the species reported to have eaten masks. In one instance, in the Netherlands, a small European perch became trapped in the thumb of a discarded latex glove.

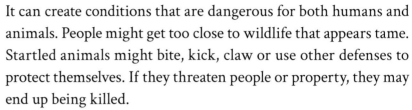

This pigeon risks injury or death if the debris attached to it becomes tangled in other objects and restricts its movements. If string around a toe or leg cuts off circulation, the bird may lose that body part. PIL-ART/SHUTTERSTOCK.COM

PETER VERREUSSEL/DREAMSTIME.COM

JDZACOVSKY/SHUTTERSTOCK.COM

ANIMAL SPOTLIGHT: *Land Mammals*

Around the world, news outlets report on animal encounters with litter. In the Netherlands a fox was saved after getting its head stuck in a corn-chip bag. In England a fox needed a tin can wriggled off its head. In Canada rescuers removed an elastic from a red squirrel's neck. People have saved animals from jars, bubble-lid cups and plastic six-pack rings.

Across North America, coyotes are adapting to living in cities, where they take advantage of **anthropogenic** food sources. In Edmonton, AB, a team of researchers examined the stomach contents of urban coyotes. They found plenty of food scraps, including a fully wrapped burrito. Human foods make coyotes more likely to suffer from disease and carry **parasites**. Coyotes

in poor condition capture less prey because they have less energy for hunting. This leads them to depend on anthropogenic food, which leads to more frequent aggressive encounters with people.

Larger mammals struggle with litter too. Bears have gotten their heads stuck in buckets and barrels. In Canada's Kootenay National Park, a mother grizzly bear and two cubs were spotted licking a sardine can and playing with litter in a ditch. Species that seek food along highways are more likely to step onto pavement and get hit by cars.

Litter Can Harm Any Animal

In Great Britain a roe deer was spotted with a plastic garbage bag stuck on its antlers. The bag blocked his sight from one eye. In another

incident, the antlers of two deer became tangled in the same rope. Animals caught in rope, string, nets or fishing line can become more snarled as they try to break free. Tangling can make it hard or impossible for them to move and care for their young. Not being able to find or eat food can lead to starvation. (The two deer tangled in the same rope died.)

Mammals like mice, shrews and voles face a different type of hazard. Tiny enough to climb into drink bottles and cans, they become trapped. Researchers estimate about 2.9 million small mammals die in metal cans and glass bottles every year. You might think of these critters as pests, but they are important members of the **food chain**.

FINES OF $5500 APPLY

Animal waste leaves behind nutrients and bacteria that can reach storm drains and enter local waterbodies. Nutrients increase algae and weeds. Bacteria can cause illness and make water unusable to people who want to swim, boat and fish.
CLARANILA/GETTY IMAGES

WHO'S IN CHARGE OF LITTER?

No matter where you live, there's bound to be litter. There's also sure to be people trying to stop the problem. *Municipal* governments are responsible for managing trash. Cities and towns make choices about whether to run recycling and compost programs. They decide where to place public garbage cans and *landfills*. Municipal governments often try to educate people about litter's harm. They may erect signs and charge fines to discourage littering. While municipal governments deal with local problems, the United Nations Environment Programme (UNEP) tackles this issue across the planet.

The *United Nations (UN)* sets important goals to reduce land-based and marine pollution and ensure a healthy environment. UNEP encourages nations to strengthen their environmental laws.

No Idea Is Too Crazy

The wet season on the Indonesian island of Bali is nicknamed "garbage season" because of the tons of refuse that wash ashore. In 2009 three Balinese teens founded Make A Change Bali to clean up plastic pollution. Sam, Gary and Kelly were 12, 14 and 16 years old, respectively, when they began removing trash from beaches. Unfortunately, more plastic always appeared, threatening sea turtles, coral reefs and other marine species.

The siblings' motto is "No idea is crazy enough to change the world." That's why, in 2017, Sam and Gary climbed into kayaks made of plastic bottles. They paddled through one of Earth's most polluted waterways—Indonesia's Citarum River. In some places garbage made it hard to see the water, and dead fish, goats and other animals floated amid the trash. The pollution had killed almost 60 percent of the river's fish species. Sam and Gary's videos caught the attention of Indonesia's president, who launched a seven-year cleanup project to restore the country's most polluted waterways.

In 2020 the trio launched Sungai Watch to clean rivers. The organization uses floating barriers, called booms, to prevent garbage from floating down rivers and being swept to the ocean. In their first year, 100 booms in 92 rivers stopped 298 tons (263 metric tons) of plastic from reaching the sea.

ALEKS333/SHUTTERSTOCK.COM

It promotes ways to reduce waste and harmful substances in the environment, including litter. UNEP also works to help manage and restore **ecosystems,** which results in safer wildlife habitat.

People in power have important roles to play when it comes to tackling litter problems. Fortunately, you don't have to sit back and wait to see how things go. You're in charge of trash too! After all, you make decisions about your own garbage every day. For example, you might choose to use reusable cloth masks to generate less rubbish. You might remind people to pull the elastic loops off disposable masks before placing the waste in a trash bin. Each day offers new opportunities to find ways to reduce littering and help protect animals whether they live in cities, on farms or in the wild.

When cleaning up litter, put safety first. Wear protective gloves or use a garbage grabber to protect yourself from direct contact with germy trash. STOCK-ASSO/SHUTTERSTOCK.COM

NO MESS, NO STRESS

If you're like me, discovering how trash harms animals makes you feel frustrated, but there is good news. Littering is a problem that can be solved. As you'll see, we can find better ways to prevent the mess by examining why people leave garbage behind. We can uncover the most effective ways to clean up by looking at what happens to trash after it falls from a person's hand. As more people learn about the ways litter hurts pets, farm animals and wildlife, more solutions will be found. Perhaps one day there will be fewer news stories about animals needing rescue.

MOUNT A CAMPAIGN

One way to fight litter is to let people know how it impacts animals. Pick a local park, natural area or waterbody. Gather some friends and create posters or videos showing how different species are affected. Promote simple solutions such as carrying your trash home or to the nearest bin.

Activist Rob Greenfield wanted to find an unforgettable way to draw attention to the daily waste that humans create and then forget about. His solution was to wear all the garbage he generated over 30 days! SIERRA FORD PHOTOGRAPHY

CHAPTER TWO

Where Litter Is Born

A LOOK AT LITTERBUGS

Litter can lead to fire and other safety hazards. It can lower the value of houses and discourage people from entering businesses. The United States spends about $11 billion on litter removal each year.
CGN089/SHUTTERSTOCK.COM

Casual Littering

Litter is usually present anywhere people walk, drive or hang out. It is easy to spot outside convenience stores and malls and around loading zones, where stores receive their stock deliveries. It is common at construction sites, sporting events and parking lots. You may have noticed that garbage builds up at transition points, such as bus stops and store entrances. People at these busy spots often break littering laws to follow other rules, such as no food or drinks inside.

Putting trash in the right place is always a good choice. It's not even hard. So what's going on? Why do people drop unwanted items on the ground? Researchers say litterers often admit to being lazy. Some claim they couldn't find a trash can or ashtray. Others seem to make their own rules. They may litter when alone, but not if someone is looking. They might drop

Outdoor events can create littering hot spots. Some communities organize Adopt-a-Street programs. They supply trash bags, gloves, and other supplies to volunteers who agree to pick litter along a stretch of road. LUCAS NINNO/GETTY IMAGES

trash on city streets but not in a forest or other natural place where they feel a greater respect for their environment. People in cities don't tend to think about the consequences to pets or wild animals, especially if they don't frequently notice them.

Often litterbugs come up with excuses to make their actions seem less wrong. Someone watching a football game, for example, might say, "It's okay to drop trash here because someone is paid to clean it up. People have jobs because of litter." Of course, littering is never a respectable behavior and these reasons are not acceptable. Animals can get to refuse before it is gathered. Garbage can blow outside the area being cleaned, becoming a hazard to animals and the environment.

Deliberate Littering

Have you ever noticed piles of faded car tires or bulging bags of garbage in strange places? You might spot lumber scraps or other construction rubbish along roads or in ditches. Maybe you've seen broken furniture, appliances or mattresses in a parking lot. Sometimes people get rid of bulky trash by dumping it on

As well as posing a safety hazard, roadside debris impacts flora and fauna along transportation routes. It may enter stormwater systems and block, flood and pollute drainage systems and waterways. ROBERT BROOK/GETTY IMAGES

public or private property. This deliberate, unlawful disposal of unwanted items is called *fly dumping* or *fly tipping* because it is done "on the fly" or "on the move." Often fly-dumpers want to avoid paying fees at landfill sites. Illegal dumping also happens for the same reason as casual littering—laziness. And sometimes people tip trash because they live in places without garbage pickup or facilities to manage unwanted items.

Illegal dumping creates hazards. As you'll read in chapter 3, toxic substances in the waste can contaminate soil, land and waterbodies where animals live. People leaving trails and roads to look for places to dump their refuse can damage delicate habitat, which may not recover. Children exploring rubbish can become trapped in old freezers or refrigerators. If a load of garbage blocks a culvert, creek or other drainage system, flooding can occur, forcing animals to flee dens, nests and feeding areas. Sometimes people set fire to trash piles. This illegal act, called arson, is extremely dangerous. If aerosol cans, gas containers or propane tanks are present, explosions can occur. Fires can spread beyond rubbish piles, putting people, property, pets, farm animals and wildlife at risk.

It doesn't take much wind for lightweight bags to sail out of landfill sites. Managers can reduce blowing waste by controlling the spread of debris at dumping zones. ZELJKOSANTRAC/GETTY IMAGES

GUESS THE MESS

How many different types of litter do you spot?

Answer: Seven—plastics; metals; food; paper products; beverage containers; chemical residue; and mixed waste, including cigarette butts, a blister pack and other items made up of two or more components.

WASTE WOES

Have you ever wondered what happens to the unwanted items you put in garbage cans? If you live in a community with waste-management laws, it is probably delivered to a landfill site. Landfills are meant to reduce trash's impact on the environment. Rubbish sent there seems to have safely "gone away," but wind often spreads litter to land and sea habitats. In addition, the plastic liners of aging landfills can leak, allowing more **contaminants** to enter the environment.

If you live somewhere without an organized system to deal with garbage, you have to get rid of it yourself. People in low-income countries usually take their refuse to open dump sites. Blustery weather spreads litter, which attracts flies, rats and other animals. People may burn their household trash too. These "solutions" create pollution and other hazards that affect people, as well as animals that come to feed on the trash.

Cities, towns and other communities maintain fleets of garbage trucks to transport their waste to landfill sites. New York City operates 2,000 garbage trucks daily! Some of its trash is delivered to sites as far away as South Carolina.
DALIBOR DANILOVIC/SHUTTERSTOCK.COM

IS THIS LITTERING?

	YES	NO
Release a balloon into the air.	☐	☐
Drop a candy wrapper under your seat at a movie theater.	☐	☐
Toss a soda can into a ditch, expecting someone to collect it for the recycling deposit.	☐	☐
Set unwanted items beside an overflowing garbage bin.	☐	☐
Fail to use animal-proof bins or take other steps to prevent creatures from getting into your trash.	☐	☐
Leave shotgun shells on the ground.	☐	☐
Dump fish guts on a riverbank.	☐	☐
Ignore paper that blows out a car window.	☐	☐
Leave a carcass behind when hunting.	☐	☐
Drop a fishhook in a lake or river.	☐	☐
Release paper lanterns into a waterbody.	☐	☐
Add a Christmas tree with tinsel still on it to a compost pile.	☐	☐

Littering is any action that leaves trash where it does not belong.
If you answered yes to every statement, you're a littering expert!

Chinese sky lanterns can contain paper, cloth, string, wires or bamboo and be lit with candles or fuel cells. They may float long distances through the air or over waterways before becoming litter that threatens livestock and wildlife if they aren't retrieved. ADISORNFOTO/SHUTTERSTOCK.COM

KAREN MASON

ANIMAL SPOTLIGHT: *Birds*

Like other animals, birds may eat litter or become tangled in trash. With beaks instead of teeth, however, many birds must eat grit to help break down the things they eat. When game birds like grouse, quail, pheasant, turkeys and doves forage for food, they willsometimes eat **lead shot** from shotgun shells, mistaking it for grit. **Lead** is highly toxic and causes lead poisoning.

Lead is also used to make fishing lures and weights. Fish-eating species of birds can be poisoned if they catch a fish with lead fishing gear snagged in its mouth or body. Ducks and other waterbirds that feed on pond bottoms may swallow fishing weights and shot. Birds exposed to high levels of lead can die rapidly without showing any signs of lead poisoning. A study on trumpeter swans in Canada found that 90 percent of the birds examined had lead in their bloodstreams.

In 1991 the United States made it illegal to use lead shot when hunting waterfowl. Other countries have made similar rules, but lead continues to enter the environment from lead ammunition used in target shooting and other types of hunting, as well as from waste objects such as lead-acid batteries.

MILOS MOMCILOVIC/SHUTTERSTOCK.COM

Chasing Litter

Sometimes birds seek litter. You may have noticed gulls in populated areas looking for dropped food. Birds that chase litter may become prey to coyotes, foxes or other predators that also scavenge litter. Those that eat processed foods or moldy litter can become sick. When litter makes birds feel too full to seek out a natural diet, they will lose weight, which can put their health at risk. Birds that mistake plastics for foods will die if sharp-edged objects pierce their internal organs.

Litter also leads to problems when it's used in nest building. Birds that weave bits of plastic into their nests create dangerous homes for their young. Unnatural building materials can tangle or trap fragile chicks. Elastic bands can wrap around beaks, making eating impossible. Birds that swallow rubber bands can choke.

PREVENTION IS BEST

If you spot a bird or other animal in distress, seek help from a wildlife rehabilitation center or government department for natural resources. Wildlife rehab centers provide first aid to injured wildlife and care for wild birds and other animals until they are well enough to return to nature. These nonprofit centers, however, usually work with limited funding. They can't help every animal. To spare species from becoming ill or injured

AROUND THE WORLD

Recycling creates material that can be reused. Upcycling, however, creates new items with a greater value. In Nepal an organization called Moware Design is using waste found in the Himalayas and Kathmandu Valley to make high-quality products, such as glassware from beer and wine bottles. It uses trash to make cash!

MOWARE DESIGN

in the first place, people must stop littering. Communities must find ways to manage their garbage more effectively. Otherwise, litter will continue to harm the habitats animals depend upon. Garbage on the ground will make it harder for land species to get what they need. Rubbish will travel to the world's oceans, where cleanup and animal rescue become even more difficult. Trash that is "removed" through burning will pollute the air.

Mount Everest—the World's Highest Garbage Dump

Every year 600 people flock to the Himalayan Mountains to scale Mount Everest—Earth's highest peak. The mountains are home to 940 bird species and more than 280 types of mammals, including red pandas and snow leopards. Their waterways support 316 types of fish.

Each climber creates about 18 pounds (8 kilograms) of waste. Because it is so difficult to conquer the mountain, trekkers discard climbing gear, tents, batteries and food waste to avoid carrying extra weight. Not all climbers survive. Removing their bodies is dangerous and costly, and more than 280 human bodies now litter the mountain. As *climate change* causes some of the mountain's snow and ice to melt, more bodies and garbage appear.

Pollution is a threat to wildlife diversity in the Himalayas. Trash that enters waterways affects ecosystems as well as human drinking water. Efforts are being made to clean up Mount Everest. In 2014 Nepal's government began collecting a $4,000 (US) deposit from foreign climbers. Visitors who carry out 18 pounds (8 kilograms) of trash get their money back. In 2019 a cleanup campaign collected 22,897 pounds (10,386 kilograms) of trash. Guinness World Records lists it as the "largest cleanup on Everest."

ASHISHSHARMA1980/SHUTTERSTOCK.COM

CHAPTER THREE

Waste in the Wild

The smell of decomposing liquids or carcasses in littered bottles attracts insects. Ants may bring soil inside, make tunnels and lay eggs. Insects can become trapped in bottles, making this unnatural setting a poor choice for nesting.

THIS HABITAT IS MY HOME

Imagine what your life would be like if you could only eat foods and use materials that were available within walking distance of where you live. As humans, we typically enjoy more options. Farmers plant crops, ranchers raise livestock and countries trade goods. We earn money and buy things. Animals, however, have to use what exists within their habitats. In natural conditions they can meet their needs. The problem is that litter creates unnatural conditions.

Trash on the ground can prevent plants from completing their life cycles from seed to flower to fruit. That will leave animals with fewer resources. Suppose a soda cup falls over a one-inch spruce seedling. The cup blocks the sunlight the plant needs to grow. It diverts rain away from the seedling's roots. If the cup covers the tree too long, it will grow weak and die.

Without litter, the spruce seedling could have grown into a tree. It would have provided habitat for birds, squirrels, hares and other species.

Large amounts of dumped rubbish cause even more harm. Picture scraps of crumbling drywall, fiberglass and metal dropped in a *boreal* forest. The debris crushes and smothers both seedlings and larger vegetation—blueberry bushes, honeysuckle, beaked hazelnut, willow and other greenery. Wildlife may no longer be able to access plants they need for food, shelter and nest-building materials. Bees are left with fewer flowers to make honey. Butterflies and hummingbirds have less nectar to feed on. Deer, moose and other species lose the *browse* they eat. Squirrels miss out on nuts and cones. Other mammals, as well as birds, find fewer seeds and berries. Below ground, root eaters must seek food elsewhere.

Around the world, youth are recognizing the global litter problem and leading efforts to clean their neighborhoods and parks as well as forests, beaches, waterways and other natural areas. FILMSTUDIO/GETTY IMAGES

THE DECAY FACTOR

Litter can remain in a habitat a long time if it contains materials that do not decay easily. Cardboard cups like the one dropped over the spruce seedling are usually coated with plastic. The coating makes the cardboard waterproof and stops it from falling apart in your hand. Plastic-coated cups are *nonbiodegradable*. Organisms like *bacteria*, *fungi*, mold, earthworms, beetles and ants cannot break them down. Cups made from organic materials like 100 percent recycled paper decompose more easily. Organic waste is biodegradable because it can break down into soil and other compounds found in nature.

Decaying trash can leach toxic substances, or contaminants, into land and water environments. Batteries, for example, release such pollutants as lithium, mercury and lead. Pollution affects plant growth, the soil's ability to filter water and biodiversity. These impacts put habitat, and the creatures that live there, at risk.

You might wonder, Can't animals just find somewhere cleaner to live? Unfortunately, habitat within reach may be just as polluted. And it may already be taken! Animals guard their *territories* against members of the same species to protect the food, water, shelter and other resources they need. Animals that travel to a new habitat put a strain on the species already using it. This can cause ecosystems to experience the negative effects of crowding and competition.

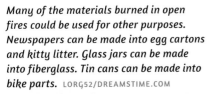

What do you call someone who picks up litter while jogging? A plogger! The word pairs jogging with plocka upp—the Swedish phrase for "pick up." Ploggers clean nature and neighborhoods while adding squats, stretches and lifting to their workouts.
EVGENY HARITONOV/SHUTTERSTOCK.COM

Many of the materials burned in open fires could be used for other purposes. Newspapers can be made into egg cartons and kitty litter. Glass jars can be made into fiberglass. Tin cans can be made into bike parts. LORG52/DREAMSTIME.COM

HOW LONG DOES MARINE DEBRIS LAST?

How long does it take objects to decay in a marine environment? It depends on their exposure to sunlight, rain, air, living organisms and other factors.

apple core—2 months

waxed carton—3 months

newspaper—6 weeks

plastic grocery bag—1 to 20 years

cigarette butt—1.5 to 10 years

plastic bottle—450 years

disposable diaper—450 years

monofilament fishing line—600 years

You may come across plastic items advertised as biodegradable but these may only break down in seawater or industrial compost facilities. Disposal in regular waste bins won't necessarily lead to biodegradation. It's important to research products before purchasing. DMITRIY SIDOR/GETTY IMAGES

The Great Pacific Garbage Patch

Plastics in oceans tend to collect in large patches that form in *gyres*. As rotating sea currents pull objects in, garbage patches grow and cloud the water. They may stretch several yards below the surface or right to the ocean floor. Barnacles, crabs and other marine species can travel long distances on garbage patches and invade habitats they would not otherwise reach. *Invasive species* upset ecosystems if they outcompete *native species* for food, space and other resources. The Great Pacific Garbage Patch—located between California and Hawaii—is the largest collection of ocean debris. Estimated to be twice the size of Texas, sampling reported in 2018 showed it to contain roughly 88,000 tons (79,000 metric tons) of plastic. Mostly made up of *microplastics*, with fishing gear and other larger objects mixed in, the garbage patch is like a difficult-to-see murky soup. The litter it contains is outside the boundaries of any country. This means no nation will pay to clean it up. Many organizations and individuals, however, work to protect marine wildlife by stopping the Great Pacific Garbage Patch and other collections of debris from growing. They organize beach cleanups, engineer machinery that can scoop up trash and encourage consumers to only support businesses with ocean-friendly practices.

KWANGMOOZAA/SHUTTERSTOCK.COM

27

POLLUTION: FROM LAND TO SKY

If you like spending time outdoors, you may have heard the motto "Leave only footprints." Picking up litter is a great way to clean our world. Sometimes, though, people get rid of the objects they collect by lighting them on fire. Poof! Trash is turned to ash. It seems like the problem is solved. Instead a new one is created. Burning transfers land pollution to the sky.

Litter typically contains plastics, chemically treated paper and other **synthetic** materials. When artificially produced objects are burned, they release pollutants into the air, including **dioxins**. These long-lasting toxic chemicals land on plants and soil. They pollute our food when they settle on garden vegetables, fruit trees and crops. Farm animals and wildlife that eat dioxin-covered plants bring poisons into the food chain.

Scattering ash in a garden, or burying it, can spread arsenic, mercury, lead and other pollutants. Harmful substances that reach ground and surface water can contaminate sources used by both animals and humans. People who ingest or inhale dioxins and other smoke pollutants can experience lung disease, heart issues and other health problems. Animals face similar issues.

PUT OUT THE FIRE

Sometimes people argue that it is okay to burn trash. They say it will get burned anyway in an incinerator at a waste-management facility. Modern incinerators, however, use pollution-control systems. They burn garbage at higher temperatures to convert dioxins into other compounds and treat ash to make it less toxic. Litter burned in a pile or backyard barrel, however, releases pollutants near the ground, where they are more likely to cause problems. Smoke makes it harder for animals to spot or smell the foods they seek. Birds are especially sensitive to smoke because they absorb oxygen while breathing in and out.

Burning trash is unlawful in some communities. When allowed, rules usually exist. Permits may allow the burning of brush but not rubber, plastic, oil, tires, carpet or furniture. Governments often promote green solutions like mulching leaves or composting organic waste. OLJENSA/GETTY IMAGES

More than 40 percent of garbage generated around the world is burned in open piles. Studies suggest carbon dioxide is the main gas released. ARUN ROISRI/GETTY IMAGES

Burning refuse releases **carbon dioxide** into the atmosphere. Carbon dioxide is called a **greenhouse gas** because it traps heat in Earth's atmosphere. The trapped heat contributes to **global warming**. Rising temperatures are a concern for many reasons, including their impact on animal habitat. Plastics also contribute to climate change because of the carbon they emit when they are made, processed for recycling and incinerated.

You can help lower the impact of carbon dioxide on the environment by reducing your use of plastics and discouraging the burning of litter. Be creative! Pack your lunch in a reusable bag. Say no to straws, plastic utensils and disposable water bottles. Choose cloth napkins over paper and reusable shopping bags over plastic. Recycle whenever possible. The best way to protect animals is to avoid creating trash in the first place.

In earlier decades, household trash contained mostly paper and wood. Today's daily waste is also made up of synthetic materials such as plastics, leather, rubber and other things that release pollutants when burned. SUNNY GORG/DREAMSTIME.COM

TRAVELING TRASH

Litter rarely stays in one place forever. Wind scatters it and rain washes it down storm drains, allowing it to reach wetlands, lakes and other waterways. Over time streams and rivers sweep garbage to the world's oceans. Experts estimate 80 percent of ocean debris comes from land. Rubbish from beach users, boaters and **offshore drilling platforms** adds to the problem.

Any piece of trash dropped on the ground may reach the nearest waterbody through a storm drain. This is hazardous because stormwater is not treated. Along with urban litter, storm-drain systems carry chemicals, pesticides, bacteria, pet waste and other pollutants. DONALD KATCHUSKY/DREAMSTIME.COM

BILLY HUSTACE/GETTY IMAGES

Scientists estimate that the amount of microplastics in Earth's upper oceans—the first 2,297 feet (700 meters)—equals about 30 billion 17-ounce (500 ml) plastic water bottles. ULADZIMIR ZUYEU/GETTY IMAGES

Trash in water may float on the surface, become suspended or sink. Over time it degrades from the effects of sunshine, wind and other weathering processes. Waves and tides break down litter too. These forces cause pieces of trash to rub together or strike sandy and rocky shores. Plastic—the most common type of marine litter—breaks down into smaller and smaller bits. Pieces about the size of a sesame seed are called *microplastics.*

Some plastics—called microbeads—start out teeny. Found in face cleansers, toothpastes and other products, they are too tiny to be caught by wastewater filtration systems. Microbeads that go down the drain enter lakes, rivers and seas.

Microplastics and other trash that float on or near the ocean's surface stop sunlight from reaching the water below. This affects ***algae*** and other types of ***phytoplankton***, which use sunlight to help them produce nutrients. Phytoplankton form the base of the aquatic food chain. Litter that blocks sunlight leaves less food for fish, sea turtles and other species that eat plankton.

Microplastics of all kinds are found in every environment. This includes Arctic snow, mountain soils, sandy beaches and the air around us. They have even been found in human organs!

SINKING LITTER

The United Nations Environment Programme (UNEP) estimates that 70 percent of marine litter eventually sinks to the ocean floor. This trash pollutes ***sediment***—material that settles on the seabed after entering the ocean via wind, rivers and ice. Sediment is habitat to oysters, sea stars and sea squirts, as well as worms, clams and other creatures. These species, called ***benthic*** organisms, are not able to move very far—or at all. They cannot escape when pollutants from refuse leach into their habitat or when decaying garbage reduces oxygen levels. Nor can they avoid microplastics that settle on the ocean floor. Oysters, sea squirts, clams, coral, barnacles and other *filter feeders* consume plastic when they eat.

Larger types of rubbish are hazards too. Tires, sheets of metal and fishing weights can damage sensitive marine habitat like coral reefs. Glass and other jagged objects that sink to the bottom of waterbodies can injure aquatic species. Small or large, litter impacts marine habitat in every part of the world.

REACH DOWN, PICK UP

Many organizations are working to stop the flow of litter into oceans. An Australian organization called Take 3 for the Sea asks people to remove three pieces of rubbish whenever they visit a beach or other waterbody. This program, which includes participants in 129 countries, leads to the removal of 10 million pieces of refuse every year. When it comes to protecting animals from trash, small actions and community initiatives really do add up!

Marine debris can become a navigation hazard that damages vessels and endangers human health and safety. It can interfere with people's ability to support themselves through maritime industries such as fishing and tourism. ROSEMARY CALVERT/GETTY IMAGES

 AROUND THE WORLD

Meet Professor Trash Wheel. Trash wheels collect and remove garbage from water. Known by Baltimore locals as Mr. Trash Wheel, Professor Trash Wheel and Captain Trash Wheel, these trash interceptors prevent litter from entering the Baltimore Inner Harbor, Chesapeake Bay and the Atlantic Ocean. In Maryland, these three machines have collected more than 12 million cigarette butts, 750,000 plastic bags, 1.3 million plastic bottles, 1.3 million foam containers and 5,000 sports balls.

ADAM LINDQUIST/WATERFRONT PARTNERSHIP OF BALTIMORE

ANIMAL SPOTLIGHT: *Marine Wildlife*

Every year roughly 220 million tons (200 million metric tons) of plastic are produced. Eight million tons (7.25 million metric tons) end up in seawater! The United Nations Educational, Scientific and Cultural Organization (UNESCO) reports that plastics kill more than a million seabirds and more than 100,000 marine mammals every year.

Some aquatic mammals, such as dolphins and toothed whales, identify food through **echolocation** and may mistake plastic bags for jellyfish. Turtles love jellyfish and are fooled by plastic bags too. The bags can choke these animals and block their digestive systems. Aquatic species may be injured or killed if sharp plastics poke holes in their stomachs, lungs or other internal organs. Animals with trash stuck inside their bodies won't have space in their stomachs for food. This can lead to starvation. Over time whales may ingest great amounts of garbage. In Scotland a 10-year-old whale was found with 220 pounds (100 kilograms) of refuse in its digestive system.

Plastics Don't Belong in Food Chains

Plastics often enter aquatic food chains through tiny **zooplankton**, some so small they can only be seen by using a microscope.

Zooplankton are an important food source to many species. These weak swimmers feed on algae. When zooplankton mistake plastics for food, they're left without the energy they need to grow and reproduce. Plastics in water absorb chemicals from oil, pesticides and other pollutants. They're passed up the food chain as mussels, oysters, fish, whales and other species ingest tiny zooplankton. While one of these organisms may only contain a little plastic, a whale that eats thousands of pounds of zooplankton a day accumulates much more.

Zooplankton grazing on algae emit a smelly chemical called dimethyl sulfide (DMS). Seabirds catching a whiff of it expect to find food. Sometimes, though, the algae they detect are growing on plastics. Instead of finding *krill*—a type of zooplankton they eat—the birds find and swallow plastic fragments. Albatrosses, which feed by skimming their beaks across the water, gather plastic as they fish, then feed it to their chicks. UNEP reports that about 40 percent of seabirds eat plastic, including penguins, pelicans, ducks, grebes, terns and auks.

Let's Fix This Problem

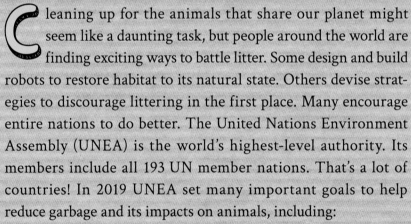

PEOPLE WITH PLANS

Street sweepers help keep roads and storm drains clear of litter and other debris. Pedestrian, cyclist and driver safety is improved when nails, glass and other hazardous litter is removed.

MIGUEL ZAGRAN/SHUTTERSTOCK.COM

Cleaning up for the animals that share our planet might seem like a daunting task, but people around the world are finding exciting ways to battle litter. Some design and build robots to restore habitat to its natural state. Others devise strategies to discourage littering in the first place. Many encourage entire nations to do better. The United Nations Environment Assembly (UNEA) is the world's highest-level authority. Its members include all 193 UN member nations. That's a lot of countries! In 2019 UNEA set many important goals to help reduce garbage and its impacts on animals, including:

- reduce the production and use of single-use plastics by 2030
- find affordable, environment-friendly alternatives to plastics
- address ecosystem damage caused by plastic products
- reuse and recycle more products
- protect and restore marine and coastal ecosystems
- improve national systems for monitoring marine litter

As well as showing that there's lots of work to do, this list offers goals anyone can work towards to help protect animals from the hazards of trash.

SENSATIONAL SOLUTIONS

People of all ages are pitching in to tackle litter in ways that will make a difference for animals and their habitats. In England, in 2016, two teen sisters founded Kids Against Plastic. Thanks to their efforts, students at more than 900 schools now use fewer single-use plastics. Another charity, called Hubbub, was removing 276 tons (250 metric tons) of trash from the Forest of Dean every year. The Hubbub team wondered if people would litter less if they felt they were being watched. They asked kids to help test an idea. Schoolchildren designed faces and local artists created them from litter found in the forest. The faces were attached to trees to "watch over" the forest. The experiment worked. People dropped 30 percent less garbage in the forest, which is habitat for deer, foxes, badgers, bats, newts and numerous other species.

In New York—a city that's home to about 1.1 million pets—Lauren Singer started a blog called *Trash is for Tossers*. She didn't just tell people to reduce their daily waste. At age 21 she set an example by choosing to live a zero-waste lifestyle. In one year she generated only one 16-ounce (454-gram) mason jar of trash.

Dutch inventor Boyan Slat was 18 when he founded a nonprofit group to help rid oceans of plastics. His organization—The Ocean Cleanup—develops technologies to remove plastics from the upper layer of garbage patches. The Ocean Cleanup has created a system to collect large objects like fishing nets and remove plastics as small as 0.04 inches (1 millimeter). Beaked whales, observed foraging in the Great Pacific Garbage Patch, are just one of the numerous species that will benefit from cleaner seas.

How many littered objects do you think you could pick in just two minutes? If you and three friends each gathered 25 pieces, you'd remove 100 pieces of rubbish from the ground. In 10 minutes, you'd gather 500 trash items. Picking litter adds up! PEOPLEIMAGES/GETTY IMAGES

This guardian of the woods demonstrates a playful, creative approach to reducing litter. Faces were installed on trees as part of a rural anti-litter campaign called Love Your Forest. HUBBUB, LOVE YOUR FOREST/HUBBUB.ORG.UK

The Bubble Barrier is a machine designed to collect plastics in rivers. It is placed on a river bottom, and then air is pumped through a tube with holes. Bubbles force plastics to the surface, and the flowing river directs the trash into a catching area. THE GREAT BUBBLE BARRIER®

MARVELOUS MACHINES

People are even inventing robots to gather litter! FRED is a solar-powered robot. His name is an abbreviation for "floating robot to eliminate debris." FRED's conveyor belt gathers floating trash ranging from 0.2 inches to 5.5 yards (5 millimeters to 5 meters) long. By going after larger pieces of refuse, the machine can remove objects before they break down into microplastics. FRED moves slowly to allow animals to get out of the way. There are plans for it to emit sound pulses that could even detect underwater objects and warn marine mammals it is nearby. Its tone would be set at a frequency that would not interfere with the underwater communication of cetaceans, such as whales and dolphins, and pinnipeds, like seals and walruses.

Wouldn't it be nice if ocean litter could find its own way into a trash can? The Seabin is a solution that might come as close as you can get. This floating rubbish collector can be used in harbors and marinas. Its underwater pump slurps water from the surface and into the Seabin through a catch net, which traps any floating marine litter. The bin bobs with the tides. It can gather about 1.5 tons (1.36 metric tons) of garbage in a year, including microplastics as small as 0.08 inches (2 millimeters) in length. This improves habitat for seabirds, fish, crustaceans, dolphins, otters and other species found in harbors and marinas.

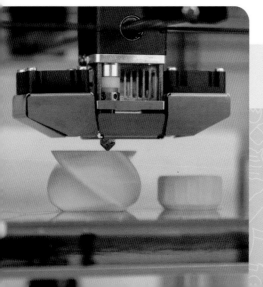

AROUND THE WORLD

The New Raw, a research and design studio in the Netherlands, uses a 3D printer to turn plastic waste into meaningful objects. It invites people to bring in their plastics to be recycled into benches, plant pots and other street furniture. A single bench uses 110 pounds (50 kilograms) of recycled plastic.

COULD YOU BE AN ANTI-LITTER ACTIVIST?

Educate

- Speak out! Prepare a speech on how littering affects animals. Now find an audience. You might talk to your class, a club or your family at the dinner table.
- Tell family members why it's important to choose food, toys and other products with less packaging.
- Encourage drivers to keep refuse containers in their vehicles to make it easy to store unwanted items and prevent them from being blown out onto the road.

Show How It's Done

- Invite friends and neighbors to join you in removing litter from your neighborhood.
- Urge your principal to host an annual schoolyard cleanup.
- Inspect your family's garbage bins to make sure animals can't get at your trash. Check that lids are secure and items can't blow away.

Call for Change

- Write a letter to the mayor of your community. Be specific about the changes you want. If your street needs bubblegum bins, ask for them!
- Suggest that coaches encourage players and fans to use reusable water bottles.
- Get published! Newspapers publish letters from citizens who want to share concerns and call for change. Read letters to the editor in your local paper to see how it's done.

COST OF WASTE

Imagine an app that detects the trash people drop and makes them pay 10 dollars for each piece of litter. If this was how society

Instead of going to a store to purchase craft supplies, look to the items you normally discard. Use your imagination to create useful or decorative items.
RONNY 80/SHUTTERSTOCK.COM

The Devon Public Library in Alberta found a novel way to encourage patrons to help keep their community clean—it lends garbage pickers as well as books!
DEVON PUBLIC LIBRARY

worked, everyone would be more careful. Instead people pay the costs of cleaning litter at tax time. That's because the task of tidying public spaces falls to governments. The money they spend comes from **taxpayers**. Every year governments are forced to spend billions of tax dollars to remove the items people leave behind.

How is all that money spent? Some is used to hire sanitation workers. They clean storm drains and remove rubbish from public lands and waterways. Governments also buy street-sweeping vehicles, bulldozers, dump trucks and other machinery and tools. They pay the salaries of law enforcement officers. They pay for signage and programs that remind people to put garbage in bins, use less plastic and recycle.

In 2019 a study in Pennsylvania found that, collectively, nine cities in the state were spending more than $68 million a year on litter. As well as removing trash, the money went toward education, prevention and law enforcement. The state used the study to develop a Litter Action Plan. It asks governments, businesses and the public to take part in reducing the problem.

Waste Pickers Make a Difference

In some developing countries, people support their families by picking trash and selling what they find. Rubbish piles up in communities without waste-disposal services. In Indonesia uncollected garbage is usually burned, tossed into canals or rivers or dumped on streets or in parks. Sometimes it is just buried. Waste that is collected is often dropped in open dumps or unsanitary landfills. Birds, goats, cats, rats and other animals scavenge for food in the refuse.

There is so much trash that more than tens of thousands of Indonesians work as waste pickers, including children helping parents. They search for electronic waste and objects that contain metal, wood or plastic, hoping to find items to recycle or sell. The workers help keep streets clean. They also turn garbage into usable products.

Picking trash, however, is a poor way for people to support their families. Waste pickers do not earn much money, and the work is dangerous. Mountains of garbage can cause deadly landslides. Pickers must avoid bulldozers and hazardous waste. Indonesia's rubbish problem would be even worse without its waste pickers, but hazards and unclean conditions put their lives at risk.

DOIDAM 10/SHUTTERSTOCK.COM

COMBATING LITTER

Special Ways

Around the world, people are finding ways to bring attention to littering and its impact on the environment. Here are some things you could do.

- Gather friends, brooms and dustpans and remove trash near storm drains. Set a goal, like clearing two storm drains per volunteer.
- Host a scavenger hunt, with a list that includes litter only. Instruct participants to wear gloves and avoid hazardous waste. Weigh the results and declare a winner.
- Find a way to turn a discarded object into something useful or decorative.

These children are crafting garbage into litter critters in front of a vehicle called the Trashconverter. It is used to encourage forest-friendly behavior by offering treats in exchange for litter. The Trashconverter attends schools and community events in England's Forest of Dean.
HUBBUB, LOVE YOUR FOREST/HUBBUB.ORG.UK

SPECIAL DAYS

March 3	**World Wildlife Day**
March 21	**International Day of Forests**
April 22	**Earth Day and the Great Global Cleanup**
May and October, second Saturday	**World Migratory Bird Day**
May 22	**International Day for Biological Diversity**
May 29	**Learn About Composting Day**
June 1–8	**World Ocean Week**
June 8	**World Oceans Day**
July 3	**International Plastic Bag Free Day**
September	**International Coastal Cleanup Month**
September 7	**International Day of Clean Air for Blue Skies**
September, third Saturday	**World Cleanup Day and US National Cleanup Day**
September, fourth Sunday	**World Rivers Day**
October, fourth Saturday	**Make a Difference Day**
On/near November 15	**America Recycles Day**
December 5	**World Soil Day**
Schools are encouraged to pick any date that suits them annually	**No Litter Day**

ANIMAL SPOTLIGHT: *Pets and Farm Animals*

If you've ever seen a dog pulling on its leash, you know how determined canines can be when something smells interesting. They may wolf down littered food or other objects before you can stop them. Eating trash can cause dogs and cats to get garbage *toxicosis*, a condition often called garbage gut. Moldy bread and cheese are common culprits, but many other foods are harmful too. Dogs that eat litter containing xylitol can experience liver injury or failure.

Sandra Rhodes, a veterinary technician in Alberta, has helped a lot of pets after run-ins with litter. She describes dogs with cut paw pads from walking on broken glass or jagged metal. One mixed-breed dog needed golf balls removed from its stomach. A miniature pinscher got its head stuck in a foil chip bag and suffocated. Another dog swallowed plastic bread clips, which damaged its intestine. There have been dogs who have eaten toys, underwear, nylons, balls, socks, barbecue skewers and badminton birds. Sandra said both cats and dogs have needed to be treated after swallowing thin plastic wrap. Cats were brought into the clinic after eating yarn, greasy strings used to tie roast beef, and tinsel left outside on Christmas trees. She advises pet owners to always be aware of hazards their animals might encounter.

Protecting Cows and Horses

When litter blows onto farmland, animals can reach it before people are aware it's there. Horses and cows may eat rubbish when grazing or consume litter that lands in their food. Livestock have died from ingesting plastic bags, string and other garbage. Sometimes the litter originates on the farm—pieces of twine or the netting used to hold hay bales together. Trash can clump into a hard mass in an animal's stomach. A blockage may lead to illness or death.

People on farms manage their own waste, and sometimes garbage piles up. Livestock may eat or injure themselves on hazardous objects. Some waste—discarded batteries, machinery, shingles and engine oil—contains lead. Cows are especially attracted to the salty taste of batteries, and a single automotive battery can kill more than one animal. Livestock that eat rubbish can produce meat that is unsafe for humans to eat. Cows may produce milk that contains pollutants. While these products won't reach store shelves in countries with safety standards, better waste management would prevent animals from being exposed to these dangers.

Agricultural organizations offer land users advice on how to compost, recycle and reduce trash in safe ways. No burning or burying! Around the world, children and young adults take part in agricultural projects as members of 4-H clubs. They tackle problems, including litter, in both cities and rural communities in more than 50 countries.

A LITTER-FREE TOMORROW STARTS TODAY

Walking down a street or through a park, you notice garbage. You may still question why people don't put litter in its place. Instead of feeling helpless, though, you have facts to share and actions to take. Set an example. Educate others. Join the many people around the world who are working to find solutions and help prevent the many ways litter hurts animals.

PETS GETTING BIT? LITTER ISN'T HELPING

Mosquitoes can pass heartworm parasites to dogs, foxes, wolves and raccoons. All they need is standing water to lay their eggs in or near. Any amount will do—even the rainwater that collects in littered cups, old tires and other trash. Some species can go from egg to adult in a soda bottle!

IS THIS RUBBISH?

TRUE OR FALSE?

Litter can cause car accidents. If you're thinking true, you're right! Boxes, lumber and other garbage may fly into windshields or pierce tires and lead to collisions if drivers swerve or brake unexpectedly. Keep America Beautiful estimates that in the United States almost 24 billion pieces of trash can be found along roads.

DIMABERLIN/SHUTTERSTOCK.COM

Acknowledgments

For years the trash found in animal habitats and all the other places it doesn't belong has troubled me. Each news story about litter harming wildlife brought me closer to writing this book. My hurdle was to find a way to present hope for a cleaner future alongside the problem. Reading and other research often solves such problems for me. This time was no exception. I discovered countless ways people around the world work to clean our littered planet and gratefully acknowledge the innovative contributions of those mentioned in this book, along with the myriad others I could not fit in.

Connecting directly with experts on a subject always leads to fresh perspectives. I'm thankful for the kind and generous assistance provided by Sandra Rhodes, Animal Health Technologist; Dr. Michael Rhodes, Nanton Veterinary Clinic; Kyle Shanebeck, MSc; Scott Sugden, MSc, research assistant at the University of Alberta; and Sherri Cox, DVM, PhD, wildlife veterinarian at the National Wildlife Centre. My gratitude extends to Orca editor Kirstie Hudson for her keen and perceptive feedback, copyeditor Vivian Sinclair for her meticulous attention to detail, and Stacey Kondla of The Rights Factory for her enthusiasm for this project and for helping to bring my words to new audiences. I'm fortunate to be part of a strong creative community and am ever appreciative of the insights I gain from my fellow writers. A most special thank-you to my family for their loving support, and to Grant Wiens for creating just the right home atmosphere, enabling me to focus on the themes I want to explore and share.

Resources

Print

Andrus, Aubre. *The Plastic Problem: 60 Small Ways to Reduce Waste and Save the Earth.* Lonely Planet Global Limited, 2020.

Beer, Julie. *Kids vs. Plastic: Ditch the Straw and Find the Pollution Solution to Bottles, Bags, and Other Single-Use Plastics.* National Geographic Kids, 2020.

Eamer, Claire. *What a Waste: Where Does Garbage Go?* Annick Press, 2017.

Mulder, Michelle. *Trash Talk: Moving Toward a Zero-Waste World.* Orca Books, 2015.

Thomas, Isabel. *This Book Is Not Garbage: 50 Ways to Ditch Plastic, Reduce Trash and Save the World!* Random House, 2018.

Online

ORGANIZATIONS FOR KIDS

Earth Rangers: earthrangers.com

Fridays For Future: fridaysforfuture.org

Kids Against Plastic: kidsagainstplastic.co.uk

Kids F.A.C.E.: kidsface.org

Kids for Saving Earth: kidsforsavingearth.org

Roots & Shoots: rootsandshoots.org

MORE TO EXPLORE

Clean Up the World: cleanuptheworld.org

Keep America Beautiful: kab.org

Let's Do It Foundation: letsdoitfoundation.org

Litter Prevention Program: litterpreventionprogram.com

Litter Project: litterproject.com

Plastic Oceans: plasticoceans.org

UNESCO Green Citizens: unescogreencitizens.org

Zero Waste Canada: zerowastecanada.ca

Apps

Litterati

Litter CleanUp

Pirika—Clean the World

Planet Patrol

Rubbish—Love Where You Live

Glossary

algae—plantlike organisms, found chiefly in water, that have no roots, stems or leaves and make their own food through photosynthesis

anthropogenic—resulting from human influence on nature

bacteria—tiny, single-celled organisms, found everywhere around us, that can be harmful or beneficial

benthic—relating to or occurring at the bottom of a waterbody

biodegradable—able to be consumed by living things, such as microorganisms, and broken down into compounds found in nature

boreal—relating to or located in northern regions, especially the plants and animals found in northern coniferous forests

browse—the tender shoots, twigs and leaves that animals eat

carbon dioxide—a colorless, odorless gas breathed out by animals and absorbed from the air by plants; it is also formed by burning fossil fuels and is a greenhouse gas.

climate change—a long-term shift in global and regional weather and climate patterns caused by increased levels of carbon dioxide in the air due to the burning of fossil fuels

compost—matter that is disintegrating into natural elements that leave no trace in the soil

contaminants—substances that introduce undesirable elements to something, making it impure or unsafe

decompose—to break down into simpler parts, especially due to the actions of living things; to decay

dioxins—a highly toxic group of chemically related environmental pollutants

echolocation—the process of sending and detecting sound waves to locate distant or invisible objects

ecosystems—communities in the environment in which organisms interact with one another

environment—the place where humans, animals and plants live, including air, land and water; the natural world and the conditions that affect it

filter feeders—species that strain water to capture and eat tiny organisms

fly dumping (or *fly tipping*)—the deliberate, unlawful disposal of unwanted items

food chain—the order in which living things use each other for food (a plant is eaten by an insect, the insect consumed by a fish, the fish eaten by an eagle and so on)

fungi—(plural of fungus) living organisms that are neither plant nor animal, such as yeasts, molds and mushrooms

germs—tiny organisms, which scientists call *microbes*, that cause disease in a plant or animal

global warming—an increase in our planet's temperature, which contributes to long-lasting changes in Earth's weather and climate patterns

greenhouse gas—any of various gases, such as carbon dioxide and methane, that trap heat in Earth's atmosphere

gyres—giant sea currents that move like slow whirlpools and pull objects in

habituation—the process of an animal losing its natural fear of humans, often as a result of learning to associate humans with food sources

invasive species—organisms that are not native to the region where they are found and are able to live and spread easily, usually causing harm to native species and their ecosystems

krill—a type of zooplankton and the chief food of some whales

landfills—structures where garbage is buried between layers of soil and a liner separates trash from the ground

lead—a soft, dense gray metallic element that is easy to shape

lead shot—small pellets of lead used in ammunition shot from a weapon

litterbug—a person who drops trash on the ground, in water or any other place where it does not belong

malnutrition—unhealthy condition or weakness that occurs from not receiving enough nutrients or from eating food that does not contain proper nutrients

microplastics—very small pieces of plastic, 0.2 inches (5 millimeters) or less in length

municipal—relating to the government of a town or city

native species—organisms that live naturally in a particular region

nonbiodegradable—unable to be broken down into very small parts by bacterial action or other natural processes

nutrients—ingredients needed to maintain life, which provide energy and allow growth

offshore drilling platforms—structures over water, usually fixed to the seabed, that support the equipment needed to drill for oil and natural gas in the sea

parasites—organisms that live in, with or on another species

phytoplankton—microscopic plants that live in saltwater and freshwater environments

processed—altered by washing, cooking or adding fats, spices, artificial flavors and other ingredients

sediment—the silt, sand, soil and other debris that settles at the bottom of a waterbody

sustainability—relating to the practice of using methods to harvest resources that do not use up or permanently damage Earth's resources

synthetic—artificially produced, especially by chemical processes

taxpayers—people with jobs who are bound by law to hand over to government a percentage of the wages they earn

territories—the places where animals find food, nest or den, mate and raise young, which they defend against others of the same species

toxic—dangerous or poisonous to living organisms

toxicosis—a diseased condition caused by the effects of a poison

United Nations (UN)—an intergovernmental organization that aims to maintain international peace and security

urban exploiters—species that take advantage of resources that come from humans

zoonotic diseases—germs that spread from animals to humans

zooplankton—small floating or weakly swimming organisms that, along with phytoplankton (free-floating plants such as very tiny algae), are either directly or indirectly a food source and which almost all ocean organisms depend upon

Index

*Page numbers in **bold** indicate an image caption.*

activism: and art, **15**, **35**; events, 39; school projects, 37; of youth, 14, 35, 37. *See also* solutions
air pollution, 19, 23, 26, 28
algae, **14**, 30, 33, 44
animal behavior: and habituation, 11–12, 13, 44; nest building, 22, **24**
animal diseases, 10, 28, 40, 41
animal rescues, 11, 12, 13, 22–23
animal-resistant garbage bins, **12**
animals: livestock, 28, 41; pets, 10, 12, 40. *See also* wildlife
animal safety: and chemicals, 18, 26, 28, 33; entanglement, **11**, 12, 13; ingested waste, 10–12, 22, 26–27, 29–32
animal waste, **14**
anthropogenic food sources, 13, 44
artwork, anti-litter, **15**, **35**

bacteria, **14**, 26, 44
Bali, beach cleanup, 14
Baltimore, MD, 31
batteries, 21, 26, 41
bears, **12**, 13
benthic organisms, 30, 44
biodegradable waste: composting, 8, **28**, 41; defined, **27**, 44; ingested by animals, 10; organic, 26, 28
birds: entanglement, 12; feeding behaviors, 10, 21, 33; lead poisoning, 21; nesting of, 22; and plastics, 32, 33; and smoke, 28
bottles: glass, 22; plastic, 13, **24**, 27
Bubble Barrier, **34**

carbon dioxide, **28**, 29, 44
cats, 12, 40
chewing gum, **7**, 10
China, 30
Chinese sky lanterns, **20**

cigarette butts, 9, 27
climate change, 23, 29, 44
compost and composting, 8, 14, **27**, **28**, 41, 44
consumer choice, 9, 29, 30, 35
contaminants, 18, 19, 26, 28, 44
coral reefs, 14, 31
cows, 41
coyotes, 13

deer, 13
dioxins, 28, 44
disease, spread of, 10, 41
dogs, 10, 12, 40
dryer lint, 22
ducks, 10, 21, 33

echolocation, 32, 44
ecosystems, 15, 27, 44
environment: contaminants, 18, 19, 26, 28, 44; defined, 44; food wastes, 10–11, 40–41; health of, 6–7, 14–15; and plastics, 11, 18, 30–31; respect for, 17–18, 29, 39; and toxic substances, 21, 26, 41
environmental laws, 14–15

farm animals, 28, 41
filter feeders, 31, 44
fishing gear, 21, 27
fly dumping, 17–18, 44
food chains, 13, 30, 32–33, 44
food waste, 10–11, 13, 22, 40–41
forest habitat, 24–26
foxes, **11**, 13
FRED (marine robot), 36

Galat, Joan Marie, 6
garbage, disposal of, **8**, **12**
glass and metal, 12, 13, 22, 31
global warming, 29, 44

governments: goals of, 34; laws, 14–15; littering fines, 18
Great Pacific Garbage Patch, 27, 35
Greenfield, Rob, **15**
greenhouse gases, 29, 44
ground pollution, 18, 26, 28
gyres, 27, 44

habitat: cleanup campaigns, 23, 25, 35, 39; forests, 24, 26; impacts of litter, 24–33; marine, 31, 32–33
habituation, 11–12, 13, 44
highway litter, 6, 13, 17–18, 41
horses, 41
household waste: average per person, 8; disposal, **8**; dumping, 17–18; open burning, 19, 28; synthetic materials, **29**; toxic, 28
Hubbub, 35
hunting, 21

Indonesia, 14, 38
insects, 10, **24**, 25, 41
invasive species, 27, 45

Kids Against Plastic, 35

landfills: debris, **18**, 19; defined, 45; open dumps, 38; sites, 14, 18, 19; waste management, 28, 37–38
lead poisoning, 21, 45
litter: cleanup tools, **15**, 37; cost of, **16**, 37–38; defined, 8–9; food waste, 10–11, 13, 22, 40–41; roadside, 6, 13, 17–18, 41; types of, 19, 20
Litterati (app), 25
litterbugs, 9, 16–18, 20, 45
livestock, 28, 41
Love Your Forest, **35**

malnutrition, 11, 45
marine life, 29–31, 32–33
marine pollution: gyres, 27, 44; and
    oxygen levels, 31; plastics, 14,
    29–31; trash cleanup, 31, **34**, 36
marine robots, 31, 33
masks, disposable, 12, 15
mice, shrews and voles, 13
microplastics, 27, 30, 45
Mount Everest, 23
municipal governments, 14, 37, 45

native species, 27, 45
Nepal, 22, 23
New York City, **19**
nonbiodegradable, 26, 45
nutrients: and animal waste, **14**;
    defined, 45; lacking in human
    food, 10

Ocean Cleanup project, **33**, 35
oceans. *See* marine pollution
organic waste, 26, 28
otters, **9**, 36

packaging and wildlife, 11
paper products, **17**, 20, 26, 27
parasites, 13, 45
pets, 10, 12, 40
phytoplankton, 30, 45
plastics: bags, **18**, 27, 32, 34,
    35; bottles, 13, **24**, 27; and
    climate change, 29; decay of,
    27; harm to animals, 11, 29–31;
    limits to recycling, 30; marine
    pollution, 14, 27; microbeads,
    30; microplastics, 27, 30, 45;
    reduction of use, 34; six-pack
    rings, 12, 13
poisoning: lead, 21, 45; toxic
    chemicals, 11, 26, 28, 41, 45

pollution sources: ash, 28; batteries,
    21, 26, 41; burning trash, 19, 23,
    26, 28
public awareness: and burning
    trash, 28; campaigns, 15, 39;
    consumer choice, 9, 29, 30, 35;
    cost of littering, 37–38; excuses to
    litter, 16–18; and impacts of litter,
    14–15, 37; and nonbiodegradable
    items, **27**; preparing the trash, **8**

recycling: and artwork, **37**; sorting
    of, 30; upcycling, 22, **26**, 36
resources, 35, 39, 43
rivers. *See* waterways
rodents, 10, 13
rope and nets, entanglement, 12
rubber bands, 22

school projects, 37
Seabin, 36
seabirds, 32, 33, 36
sea turtles, 14, 30, 32
sediment, 30, **34**, 45
Singer, Lauren, 35
solutions: cleanup campaigns, 23,
    25, 35, 39; composting, 8, **28**, 41;
    marine robots, 31, 33, 36; picking
    up litter, **7**, 15, 25, **26**, 31; and
    prevention, 22–23, 34; resources,
    35, 39, 43; and unaddressed mail,
    17; upcycling, 22, **26**, 36; and zero
    waste, 29, 35
squirrels, 13
Sungai Watch, 14
sustainability, 9, 45
swans, 21
synthetic materials, 28, **29**, 45

Take 3 for the Sea, 31
taxpayers, 37–38, 45

technology: barriers, 14, **34**; Litterati
    (app), 25; marine robots, 31, 33, 36
tires, **9**, 31
toothpaste, microbeads, 30
toxicosis, 40, 45
toxic substances: chemicals, 18, 26,
    28, 41; defined, 45; and household
    waste, 10–12
trash. *See* litter
trash (garbage) cans, **6**, **12**, 37
Trash is for Tossers (blog), 35
trash wheels, 31

United Nations (UN): defined, 45;
    goals, 14–15, 34
United States: cost of litter removal,
    16, 38; littering fines, 18; use of
    lead shot, 21
urban exploiters, 10, 13, 45

waste management: cost of, **16**,
    37–38; debris, 18, 19; incinerators,
    28; landfills, 14, 18, 19; open
    dumps, 38
waste pickers, 38
waterways: pollution sources, **9**, **14**,
    28, **29**; trash cleanup, 14, 31, **34**,
    36
whales, 32, 35
wildlife: and food waste, 10–11, 13,
    22, 40–41; and habituation, 11–12,
    13, 44; land mammals, 13, 24–25;
    marine, 29–31, 32–33; rescues, 11,
    12, 13, 22–23; urban exploiters,
    10, 13, 45

youth: anti-litter activists, 14, 35;
    projects, **25**, 37

zoonotic diseases, 10, 45
zooplankton, 32–33, 45

JOAN MARIE GALAT is an award-winning author with more than 25 titles. She was first published at the age of 12, when she became a paid weekly newspaper columnist. After studying biological sciences, Joan worked in radio before becoming a freelance writer and editor. Her books explore nature, ecology, astronomy, engineering and other topics. Joan's books have won and been nominated for numerous awards, including the Crystal Kite, Skipping Stones, Rocky Mountain, Red Cedar, Hackmatack and Green Prize for Sustainable Literature, among others. A frequent presenter, Joan has traveled across Canada and internationally to promote literacy and deliver science-themed talks. Joan lives near Edmonton.